SPEAKING VOLUMES

SEAMUS HOSEY

Published in association with
Radio Teilifís Éireann

BLACKWATER PRESS

Editor
Anna O'Donovan

Design & Layout
Philip Ryan

ISBN
0-86121-722-5

© – Seamus Hosey 1995

Produced in Ireland by
Blackwater Press
c/o Folens Publishers
8 Broomhill Business Park,
Tallaght, Dublin 24.

INTRODUCTION

To be allowed roam the bookshelves of public people in the privacy of their own homes is a rare form of voyeurism I have enjoyed over the past few years in making the series Speaking Volumes for RTE Radio. From each encounter with the personalities reflected between these covers I have been enlightened, not just about their favourite books but also about many fascinating aspects of their more private selves. From Ian Paisley to Maureen Potter and from John B. Keane to Terry Keane, I have come away with a greater regard for the complex process by which books become part of our lives and the ways in which they inform and shape our destinies. Another personality featured in this volume, poet and professor, Brendan Kennelly, has said, 'We don't read books but books read us.' For me the experience of being confronted with the distillation of so many lifetimes' reading has been an enriching and enthralling experience. From each encounter whether it be with Seamus Heaney or Sister Stanislaus Kennedy I have come away humble at the poverty of my own reading but determined to share in the treasure house of others' riches.

I hope that this volume captures the very individual voices of the people interviewed and that not too much of the colour and verve of the spoken word has been lost in the transition from tape to page. To all those who opened, not just their homes and their bookshelves to me but also their hearts and their love of books, I offer my thanks. I hope the reader enjoys even a fraction of the pleasure and enlightenment I have had, and continue to have, in presenting the series over the years.

Seamus Hosey
Dublin 1995

ACKNOWLEDGEMENTS

I would like to thank Michael Littleton, Managing Editor of Features and Arts in RTE Radio for commissioning the Speaking Volumes series and giving me every support to develop it. I would like also to thank Michael O'Sullivan who suggested the idea of the book and Catriona O'Connell of RTE who patiently typed the manuscript and made many useful suggestions. John Cooney took many of the fine photographs and others appear courtesy of the *RTE Guide*. Finally, I would like to thank especially John O'Connor and my editor, Anna O'Donovan, of Blackwater Press for all their work and advice.

CONTENTS

1 Maeve Binchy 7
2 Bryan MacMahon 13
3 Ian Paisley 17
4 Maureen Potter 23
5 Frank McGuinness 29
6 Seamus Heaney 35
7 Hugh Leonard 41
8 Patrick Mason 47
9 Richard Murphy 52
10 Gemma Hussey 56
11 Rosaleen Linehan 61
12 Benedict Kiely 69
13 Tim Pat Coogan 73
14 John O'Conor 79
15 Nuala Ní Dhomhnaill 85
16 Terry Keane 91
17 John B. Keane 97
18 David Marcus 101
19 Gerald Davis 107
20 Helen Lucy Burke 113
21 Sister Stanislaus Kennedy 117
22 John A. Murphy 122
23 Ita Daly 127
24 Edward Delaney 133
25 Jeananne Crowley 137
26 Eamon Dunphy 143
27 David Norris 147
28 Lelia Doolan 154
29 Joe O'Connor 159
30 Paul Funge 166
31 Michael D. Higgins 170
32 Fintan O'Toole 175
33 Nora Relihan 181
34 Brendan Kennelly 187
35 Mary Leland 193
36 Sean J. White 197
37 Bob Quinn 202
38 Augustine Martin 207

1

MAEVE BINCHY

Maeve Binchy, international bestselling author and distinguished columnist with *The Irish Times*, was born in Dublin and educated at Holy Child Convent in Killiney and later at University College Dublin. After a career in teaching she joined *The Irish Times* in 1969 and has written for them from all over the world. Two of her plays for the stage, *End of Term* and *Half Promised Land*, were staged by the Peacock Theatre in Dublin and *Troubled Hearts*, based on three short stories, toured Ireland recently. Among her international bestselling novels are *Light a Penny Candle*, *Echoes*, *Firefly Summer*, *The Copper Beech*, *The Glass Lake* and *Circle of Friends* which was made into a hugely successful movie. She has also written four volumes of short stories and has had two collections of her journalism published. She is married to writer Gordon Snell.

Maeve Binchy, dividing your time as you do between Dublin and London, do you ever find that the book you desperately need to put your hands on is in the other house?

Well, I do sometimes and I think that I'm sure I had that book beside my bed, but I realise it's beside the bed in another land. Of course, it's also a great excuse when someone like you comes to my house in Dublin, I can tell you that all the really cultured and academic books are in London, that what you see here is just a common or ordinary collection and I can get away with being cultured in the other place. I had this dream once that I would live in a house where there were bookcases from ceiling to floor, and although I do have bookcases from ceiling to floor in some of the rooms and I have books in every room, they are not very well organised. There is great business of serendipity in that you look at a shelf and you find a whole lot of miscellaneous things on it. I had hoped once to have them displayed author by author and alphabetically but that is a dream, very much in the future.

The first book that catches my eye on your shelves is a book that I think has a great appeal to you as a professional writer, a book about the English language.

This is called *Mother Tongue* by Bill Bryson and I bought it in the line of duty when I was going to speak at a Writer's Day once. It's about the English language and where our words come from and I was so fascinated by it that I couldn't put it down. It was very pleasant when I met the author to be able to say 'I loved your work', and mean it, instead of the things that actors and actresses are always saying to each other: 'Darling you were wonderful!' It is full of interesting quirky explanations about words like the different attitudes nationalities have about words. Let me read you an extract.

> Here, as in almost every other area of language, natural bias plays an inescapable part in any attempt at evaluation. No one has ever said, 'Yes, my language is backward and unexpressive, and could really do with some sharpening up.' We tend to regard other people's languages as we regard their cultures – with ill-hidden disdain. In Japanese, the word for foreigner means 'stinking of foreign hair'. To the Czechs a Hungarian is a 'pimple'. Germans call cockroaches 'Frenchmen', while the French call lice 'Spaniards'. We in the English-speaking world take French leave, but Italians and Norwegians talk about departing like an Englishman, and Germans talk of running like a Dutchman. Italians call syphilis 'the French disease', while both French and Italians call con games 'American swindle'. Belgian taxi drivers call the poor tipper 'un Anglais'. To be bored to death in French is 'être de Birmingham', literally 'to be from Birmingham' (which is actually about right). And in English we have 'Dutch courage', 'French letters', 'Spanish fly', 'Mexican carwash', (i.e. leaving your car out in the rain), and many others.

The book is full of things like that and I often take it out just to read another chapter.

I happen to know that you are a Self-Improvement book freak and one of those volumes I see on your shelves is entitled 'The Secret of How to Win Freedom from Clutter'. Surely you don't need a book like that?

This book, I think, should be on every person's reading list and it should be taught in schools and I've often said that the man who wrote it, Don Aslett, should actually run the world. He has this theory that if anybody is a hoarder or a magpie as I'm inclined to be and still have essays I wrote in school thirty-five years ago, he tells you how to get rid of them. He tells you, for example, about clutter: that if you really love something so much you should photograph it and put the picture on your mantelpiece or you should cremate it and put it in a little urn. He says that everybody in the world probably has one broken watch in a drawer somewhere and why do you keep it? It's also a very moral book. There is no reason why you should keep things when other people don't have them. It gives you freedom and it manages to spread possessions round more equally. It's a marvellous book and I read it all the time, especially when I open a drawer and find it's too full.

Some of the other Self-Help books you have on your shelves I suspect you bought because of the quirkiness of their titles, like 'The Joys of Stress' or 'How To Say No When You Really Mean Yes'.

I read hundreds of these books about Management Skills and I couldn't manage myself out of a paper bag! I also read a lot of books like this one by Edwin Bliss called *Getting Things Done*. It crosses my mind that I'm very foolish to be reading these books because, after all, if you have thrived on stress in the beginning you shouldn't need *More Ways of Managing Stress*, you should be in great shape. I am, like an awful lot of people, a sucker for these kinds of books. I think if I read books about managing time my time will get managed. I don't realise that what I should actually be doing upstairs is sitting down answering the letters and finishing the articles and writing the short stories.

Lest people think you spend your time immersed in Self-Help books, you have here a huge fiction library and I see Fay Weldon featuring prominently.

I've always loved Fay Weldon. I'm amazed at the way she is able to write so much and most of what she writes is very, very good. I've met Fay Weldon and interviewed her. She's an astounding woman. She has this thin, almost babyish voice and she says the most outrageous things in a very posh accent. She says the most extraordinary things about women and men which I find very cheering and is quite over the top, of course, in her attitudes to women. She grew up in a household in New Zealand with her mother and her grandmother and her aunt and she thought that the world was ruled by women and was very surprised that other people discovered it was ruled by men. *The Life and Loves of a She Devil* is one of the most outrageous novels where a woman, to wreak terrible revenge upon a man, does the most extraordinary things.

It is very appropriate, since we are sitting here in Dalkey, that you should have Flann O'Brien's novel 'The Dalkey Archive' on your shelf.

I'm particularly tickled by the dedication of that book. He says: 'I dedicate these pages to my Guardian Angel, pressing upon Him that I'm only fooling and warning Him to see that there is no misunderstanding when I go Home.' I love that kind of attitude where he is saying he will write the most outrageous irreverent kinds of things but he wants to keep a foothold in there as well and his Guardian Angel will look after him. Well, of course anyone who works in *The Irish Times*, as I do, would be enormously proud of the man who wrote the marvellous Myles na Gopaleen column there. Any of us who tried to write a column had to put it out of our minds, it was so good. I think I like the *Third Policemen* best of all the novels but I love *The Dalkey Archive* and, of course, since every step of it is so familiar to me I often feel when I go up the Vico Road myself that I might meet an Archangel. Once, many years ago he wrote me a letter complaining about some point of grammar in a freelance article I wrote for the paper and with a red face I tore it up and dismissed him as a pedant. But I'm very sorry now that I did not keep the letter.

You are part of what is a growing cult following for the writings of Elmore Leonard.

There was a quote on the back of the first Elmore Leonard book I every read, and you know how you can't believe them, saying that when you had read your first Elmore Leonard you would rush out and buy everything he had ever written. People say they don't like the sound of a lot of violence and cops and sleazy Florida underworld gangsters who all seem to be double dealing but the language is terrific and you are drawn into a world where gangsterism is not so much acceptable as it is the only world and he describes it so well. It's an old-style fiction written in modern gangsterland.

You read a lot of your Irish contemporaries and I see William Trevor's 'Two Lives' on your shelves.

I am more jealous of William Trevor than I am of any other human being. He has the most extraordinary ability to make everything seem real: to make the big house seem real and to make the small cottage equally real. *Two Lives* is a very strange book. It's two stories about women, both very different. The first story is about this girl, Mary Louise Dillon, of a poor Protestant family in the south-east of Ireland and her very limited options of whom she could marry. She is going to marry a very dull man from the town who is within the clan but she finds escape through an ill, sickly cousin with whom she used to sit in the graveyard and read Turgenev. It's about how she went mad really.

The second story is a totally different one about a woman who runs a boarding house in Italy, and she is also mad but in different circumstances. She invites survivors of a train crash back to her house to recuperate and she weaves fantasies about their lives. Fiction changes her life also. I love John McGahern too, especially his early novel *The Barracks*. I envy his ability to transport you into a world you would never know. I've never forgotten the claustrophobia and unloving atmosphere of that novel. The people stay in your mind forever. I've read it many times since.

2

BRYAN MacMAHON

Bryan MacMahon is a man of many parts – schoolmaster, novelist, short story writer, dramatist, translator, ballad-maker and author of children's books. He has lectured widely on literature and the craft of writing and is a superb raconteur and a genial and gifted storyteller. He lives in his native Listowel, County Kerry where he taught for over forty years. His first poems and stories were published in *The Bell* literary magazine. Among his works of fiction *The Lion Tamer and Other Stories, Children of the Rainbow, The Honey Spike* (also a successful play) and *The End of the World and Other Stories* will endure. Recently he published an acclaimed volume of autobiography *The Master.* He has been closely associated with Listowel Writers' Week over the years and was conferred with an honorary Doctor of Letters in 1972.

We're in Church Street in Listowel in the home of one of our most eminent Irish Writers. We are surrounded by the books of a lifetime's reading. Bryan MacMahon, is it true you once ran a bookshop from your home here in Church Street?

During the war years when there was a great scarcity of books I ran a bookshop because I was cut off from books. Books are my life and I can get drunk on the smell of printer's ink because I spent a lot of time in a printer's workshop. I always wanted to own a bookshop and I started a branch of the Argosy Library. I selected the books with great care until suddenly I had something wonderful on my hands. I sold lots of copies of *The Bell*, which I was writing for under the editorship of Seán O' Faolain. The funny thing about bookshops is you'll always see a 'quare fellow' looking in the window; these people are like wasps at jam! They are always looking in the window to see what's happening in a bookshop and when you go out and you lure them in you have a companion for the evening. They are great company.

One of your all time favourite books has a very prominent place here on your shelves in a very handsome edition. It's 'The Crock of Gold' by James Stephens.

I meet many young Americans who come to see me here in Listowel and they squat at my feet here in the house or sit down in the Hotel and many of them come back to that wonderful book. It's a marvellous mixture of nonsense, pseudo-technology, philosophy and everything transferred in a very unusual way. I simply love that book. It's a crackpot philosophy of life but it's great. At its core it seems to be the soul grappling with the body or else paganism grappling with Christianity. Sometimes, when I fall from grace I am comforted by a sentence or a quotation from James Stephens:

> Man is a god and a brute. His head is in the stars but his feet are contented among the grasses of the field and when man forgets the beast on which he stands, there will be no more heaven and no more earth and the immortal gods shall blow this world away like smoke.

Now broken into its constituent parts, that philosophy seems to me to be very unusual. It says men will never be like gods and if they are there will be no time for the gods. We can never reach perfection but that does not prevent us from striving after it.

History is a great preoccupation of yours and in particular the story of Irish emigration to the United States and Canada. I see a book called 'A History of the Township of Emily, the County of Victoria'.

Although a lot has been written about the Irish-American emigration experience, not a lot has been written about Canada and places like Prince Edward Island which was going to be called New Ireland. A crowd of people, over 2,000, went from Cork/Kerry under the Peter Robinson Immigration in 1823 and they took up lands in Ontario. Their descendants have very Irish roots and they come here regularly. During Listowel Writers' Week I gave a lecture and I spoke of people leaving here in 1823 and going out to Ontario encountering the usual hazards of wolves, bears and snow. Now their city of 95,000 is Peterborough. Among the people who went there and travelled across a lake was a young fellow who jumped out of the boat and shouted: 'Tell your children and your children's children that I, Paddy Galvin, of Raheen in this year of 1823 was the first to set foot in the Holy Land'. When telling this story I stopped for effect – the old school master trick. Then I said, 'Will Colm Galvin please stand up?' A man stood up in the audience and I said, 'This is a direct descendent of Paddy Galvin, the young fellow in Ontario, after a hundred and sixty odd years.' He wrote a book called *The Holy Land*.

I see a well thumbed paperback of Arthur Koestler's book 'The Act of Creation' here on your shelves.

Any man who puts pen to paper should read this book. His theory is that art came out of the belly laugh because all art begins with the jester and then a sage sees it and says it should be remembered and the artist comes along and petrifies it for all time in the form of art. It is the grape becoming wine through that process of the jester, the sage and the artist. Koestler brings me to something that has preoccupied me in all my work: the harmonisation of opposites. It runs through all my stories. If I might digress, what makes Miss Piggy in the Muppets such an indelible character? She's the mating of two disparate characters, a dirty little pig and a debutante. They are superimposed upon each other. What makes a short story remarkable is the quality of indelibility. The simplest example I can give is a live lobster on a billiard table. Close your eyes and imagine a live lobster on a billiard table: they are opposites. One is angular, raw, awkward and the other is mathematically correct. After a lifetime of writing short stories I'm still reading stories from all over the world. I am fascinated by what's happening in the short story in South America, India, Africa, the Philippines. We in Ireland have a well deserved reputation for the short story. What makes a great short story? Seán O Faolain said it all once: 'You go around the world looking for stories, whoring after subjects, and you come home and you find a little incident that moves you and you put it into literature and then you'll have a short story that will be remembered when you're dead'.

3

IAN PAISLEY

Ian Paisley is the Leader of the Democratic Unionist Party in Northern Ireland and it was at their headquarters on the Ravenhill Road in Belfast that I met Dr Paisley. He showed me with great pride his library of some 14,000 volumes, all indexed and cross-referenced. His book-lined study had a picture depicting William of Orange at the Battle of the Boyne and over his desk hung a framed copy of Rudyard Kipling's poem 'If'. He admitted that it was a pleasure to relax and talk about his favourite books in between a hectic day's schedule of political interviews by NBC and BBC.

We are in Ravenhill Road in Belfast, the nerve centre of the Democratic Unionist Party and the hub of Dr Ian Paisley's world. This study is crammed with books – in fact I understand you have about 14,000 volumes between your office and your home. When did you begin collecting books?

My father had a great library. He introduced me to the fact that even though you are lowly and haven't much money every day you can walk with kings and princes of this earth: the kings of literature and the princes of the writing world. I was brought up on that philosophy and I became a reader of books, a lover of books and a collector of books.

People would expect that you would have many editions and versions of the Bible. Which is the one that is most special to you?

The 1911 Bible, known as the Authorised Version and this is a facsimile edition. I read my Bible through twice or three times in its entirety every year. Every page is marked with my notes and comments. Of course the Authorised Version is the Anglo-Saxon undefiled, the pure chaste language and a wonderful language at that. I don't like the new versions of the Bible in modern English because I don't believe they are faithful translations. I think they are more paraphrases or attempts to give the ideas of the person who produced them and write into the scriptures the doctrines that they probably want to propagate. I like the Authorised

Version because it is plain, it is straight and I believe it is faithful to the original text.

Moving away from the Bible but not too far away I see you have a well read copy of John Bunyan's 'The Pilgrim's Progress' on your shelves.

I have read John Bunyan's *The Pilgrim's Progress* more times than any book except the Bible. This pocket edition goes with me everywhere – it has just come back from South Africa. This other edition is actually bound in oak taken from the church where Bunyan worshipped. It is a wonderful book. It is a characterisation of people you meet every day. I mean, who hasn't met Madam Bubble or Mr Obstinacy and Mr Pliable? They live in the Ravenhill Road and they live in Dublin as well. It is a religious compendium because it deals with the issues of religion in a very unique way and of course it was written in prison.

You also read a lot of other religious tracts and pamphlets.

Yes, I do. This one here has had more influence on me personally than any other book I've ever read. It's called *The Rise and Progress of Religion in the Soul* written by Philip Dodridge who was a great hymn writer, and ran a school for Nonconformist ministers in Northampton. He was a great religious man. It deals with the religion that is immediate to man's nature. He says:

> When we look around us with an attentive eye and consider the characters and persons of men, we plainly see that though in the original constitution of their natures they only, of all the creatures that dwell on the face of the earth, are capable of religion.

So man is capable of religion. That book shook me to the foundations as a young man and it has been the basis of my own religious belief ever since.

History has been a particular passion of yours and I see you have hundreds of volumes on Irish and world history.

There are two books on history that I have picked out. The first is a three volume work by Reverend J. A. Wylie called *The History of Protestantism* and this is a classic work. I was highly honoured when I was asked to write the Preface to a recent two volume edition of the work when it was reprinted. This other one is Scott's *Worthies* and it tells the story of the struggle of Scotland, religiously in the Protestant sense, from John Knox right through to the Covenanters and right through to modern times. It is a classic work and has been in the homes of many Presbyterians in Scotland for years. It was one of the very first books I looked at as a boy in my father's library. I have read it many times and I have always been refreshed by it.

I notice on the wall behind you there is a copy Kipling's famous poem 'If'. Is that a particular favourite of yours?

Many a time when the battle has been tough, when the press have been doing their work of criticism and maybe even of libelling I have gone to that poem.

> If you can keep your head when all about you
> Are losing theirs and blaming it on you,
> If you can trust yourself when all men doubt you,
> But make allowances for their doubting too;
> If you can wait and not be tired by waiting,
> Or being lied about, don't deal in lies,
> Or being hated, don't give way to hating,
> And yet don't look too good, nor talk to wise:
>
> If you can talk with crowds and keep your virtue,
> Or walk with Kings – nor lose the common touch,
> If neither foes nor loving friends can hurt you,
> If all men count with you, but none too much;
> If you can fill the unforgiving minute
> With sixty seconds' worth of distance run,

Yours is the Earth and everything that's in it,
And – which is more – you'll be a Man, my son!

It puts impetus into your step and steel into your blood and backbone into your spine. You couldn't get anything better than that, could you? I like poetry. I also like Longfellow's 'The Village Blacksmith'.

Under the spreading chestnut tree
The village smithy stands;
The smith, a mighty man is he,
With large and sinewy hands;
And the muscles of his brawny arms
Are strong as iron bands.

When I was a schoolboy I used to go past a forge and I used to look in. That poem has a message for you and me.

We mentioned your interest in history and I can see from your bookshelves that you are also very interested in biography.

One of my favourite biographies is this three volume one of Lord Carson by Banks and Coleville. These are interesting volumes because the first two have Carson's signature on them dated March 1934. In fact I had a chap in with me who asked me why he didn't sign the third volume and I said to him: 'How could he when he was dead and buried by the time it came to be written?' Only an Ulsterman or an Irishman would ask you a question like that! This other biography is *The Life of Henry Cook* who was the great Irish Presbyterian leader in the past century. He has had a vast influence on my life, an orthodox man like myself holding fast to the Reformed Protestant faith. I have been inspired by reading that book. You would be interested to know that one of the more modern histories that I love was written by an Irish Nationalist Member of Parliament for Londonderry, Justin McCarthy. He wrote five volumes on the reign of Queen Victoria up to 1880 and then he wrote another volume on the Diamond Jubilee and another volume coming up to the succession of her son Edward VII. McCarthy himself took over the leadership of the Nationalist Party in the House of Commons after the fall of the Chief Parnell.

Of the making of books, it has been said, there is no end. Do you intend adding to the vast amount that has been written about you by giving us your own version of your life as an autobiography?

Well, if only I could get time – time is the great factor. When you are at the heart of events you are, in a sense, making the history that is being written. Then you are not really a good historian. Somebody else must write objectively and as they see it but I hope some day that I may be able to write some memories. There are so many things that have happened to me in my career that were interesting, exciting and some humorous that would make you laugh so hard that you would be sore. Some day I must commit those things to writing.

4

MAUREEN POTTER

Maureen Potter is one of Ireland's best known performers with a career spanning the bridge from child singer/dancer to national institution. To generations of Irish audiences she is synonymous with comedy pantomime at the Gaiety Theatre but she is also an accomplished actress across the boards. In the theatre she has played with some of the past greats – Jimmy O'Dea, Michael Mac Liammoir and Hilton Edwards. She has played opposite Siobhan MacKenna in *Arsenic and Old Lace* and was a memorable Ginnie Gogan in Joe Dowling's production of *The Plough and the Stars* in Dublin, London, Jerusalem and New York. Her theatre and cabaret performances are huge box-office successes and her wonderful creations, marvellously scripted by her husband, Jack O'Leary, are part of our Irish comic heritage.

We are in the Clontarf home of one of the best loved performers in Irish showbusiness, a woman who has given countless hours of joy and mirth to generations of Irish audiences. Maureen Potter, have you always been a reader?

Yes, I have, and I started reading when I was very young. My father was a great reader and he had a great collection of O. Henry short stories so I became very fond of that form of writing. I used to read everything I could lay my hands on from *Woman's Weekly* to *The Water Babies* which was read by firelight. I left school when I was twelve to go touring, so most of my education has been through reading. I used to go into bookshops when I was touring in England with Jack Hilton and Jimmy O'Dea and stay there for hours. When I was younger I always had a book with me backstage, but now that I'm older I wouldn't even look at a catalogue I'm so petrified before I go on.

The first book that catches my eye on your shelf is by Irish novelist, Francis Stuart.

This one by Francis Stuart is *The White Hare* and I was given a present of it about forty years ago and I have loved it ever since. It is a love story and I don't usually read love stories but this is one of the most beautiful ones ever written about young love; it's about a family just before the beginning of the Troubles and the things that happened to them. The young man Dominic fell in love with his brother's wife. He died for love in the end and they found the bones of the white hare. I bring it to bed and cry a little.

You have beside it a well thumbed copy of 'The Diary of a Nobody' by George and Weedon Grossmith. Why is that a favourite book of yours?

It's mad. Quite and utterly mad. Of its time it's really goonish. They write about absolutely nothing and the stupid things that happen and the nothingness:

> I woke with a terrible headache. I could scarcely see. The back of my neck was as if I had been given a crick. I first thought of sending for a doctor but I did not think it necessary. Then I felt faint. I went to Brown's the chemist who gave me a draught. So back at the office and had to leave to come home. Went to another chemist in the city. I got a draught. Brownish dose. Seems to have made me worse.

It's all that kind of thing. He talks about nothing. The two characters do nothing. They get invitations to balls and they don't go. It's wonderful. There are wonderful illustrations: 'Mr Lupin announces Mr Henry Irving'. I can't explain it: I think people would have to read it for themselves. It was a friend of mine, Tommy Hanly, who was a great broadcaster during the war who introduced me to it and it was his favourite book too.

Here's a book by a great old friend of yours.

Ah, yes, Michael Mac Liammoir's *Put Money In Thy Purse*. This is the hilarious story of the making of *Othello* with Orson Welles and really the trials and travails and the things they got up to and the struggles to make money to keep the film shooting are hilarious, as only Michael could tell them. Michael played Iago and he was wonderful; I had never seen him play that kind of part before. One scene they made in a Turkish bath because they couldn't afford the costumes.

You have a lot of books about the theatre on your shelves.

Act One by Moss Hart is a particular favourite of mine. It's the story of his life in the theatre and the plays he wrote with George Kaufman, and the horrors of touring in America where they open out of town and they spend weeks and weeks rewriting. We sometimes do that here, but we don't take so long. Hart and Kaufman were both part of the wonderfully bitchy set known as the Algonquin Circle which included Dorothy Parker. That brings me to another great favourite which I shared with Michael Mac Liammoir – *The Mapp and Lucia Stories* of E. F. Benson. I didn't know Michael was an E. F. Benson fan and we were working together in a pantomime when I was very young, and one day I said something like: 'As Miss Mapp might say,' and he looked at me in astonishment and said: 'Don't tell me you know Mapp!' So we used to do impressions of Mapp and Lucia across the stage at each other sometimes and he used to try and make me laugh. You know that terrible smile of Mapp with all those teeth. I loved the petty snobberies, the semi-grandeur and the marvellous characters like Quaint Irene, the painter, who wore trousers which at that time was very peculiar. I also loved Mr Georgie and his little red wig and the vanity of him trying to pretend that it was his own hair.

Here's a well battered and well read copy of James Joyce's 'Ulysses'.

It's one of my bedside books. Harry O'Donovan, who was Jimmy O'Dea's marvellous writing partner, gave it to me as a wedding present. I was in two Joyce films: *Ulysses* and *A Portrait of the Artist as A Young Man* which I enjoyed better working with a lot of old friends like T. P. McKenna. This is the original text, not one of those abridged or bowdlerised versions and this is one of my favourite passages featuring Leopold Bloom:

> Mr Bloom turned at Gray's confectioner's window of unbought tarts and passed the Reverend Thomas Connellan's bookstore. Why I left the church of Rome. Bird's Nest. Women run him. They say they used to give pauper children soup to change to protestants in the time of the potato blight. Society over the way papa went for the conversion of poor Jews. Same bait. Why we left the church of Rome? A blind stripling stood tapping the curbstone with his slender cane. No tram in sight. Want to cross. 'Do you want to cross?' Mr Bloom asked.
>
> The blind stripling did not answer. His wall face frowned weakly.
>
> He moved his head uncertainly.
>
> 'You're in Dawson Street,' Mr Bloom said. 'Molesworth Street is opposite. Do you want to cross? There's nothing in the way.'
>
> The cane moved out trembling to the left. Mr Bloom's eye followed its line and saw again the dyework's van drawn up before Drago's. Where I saw his brilliantined hair just when I was. Horse dropping. Driver in John Long's. Slaking his drouth.

Joyce goes on to think what the blind man was thinking and I thought that was absolutely wonderful. I'm very sceptical about the po-faced critics who read Joyce so solemnly because *Ulysses* is such a funny book. When RTE did that marvellous radio version that's where the humour came out. It was absolutely splendid. Talking of humour, here's one of my favourites. Stephen Leacock is a Canadian from McGill University. Before we were married, Jack O'Leary found on a bookstall *Sunshine Sketches of a Little Town* and he loaned it to me and I loved it and I said I'd love to get more of Stephen Leacock. So Jack sent to Folyes of

Charing Cross Road in London a list of fourteen Stephen Leacock titles, asking them to send us one and they sent us the fourteen! Jack was a Lieutenant in the army at the time with very little money so you can Imagine how thrilled he was. We have a Stephen Leacock library and when I met the Canadian Ambassador he was thrilled to see this and he sent me this little paperback copy. We based one of my Christy comedy sketches on a story by Stephen Leacock, the ABC boarding house geometry story.

You like poetry too?

One of the first poems I ever learned off by heart was 'The Ruba'iyat of Omar Khayyam' by Edward Fitzgerald. I loved it because it mentioned my name in one of the verses!

> After a momentary silence spake
> Some vessel of a more ungainly make;
> 'They sneer at me for leaning all awry;
> What! did the Hand then of the Potter shake?'

Another great passion of yours is cricket?

I bought the Autobiography of Neville Cardus, that great cricket writer, secondhand in McCullough's in Galway. He was just a wonderful man, a music and critic expert. In his book he gives marvellously poetic descriptions of cricket which is such a wonderful game. Cricket is one of my great passions in life and I love to read about it as much as watch it.

5

FRANK McGUINNESS

Frank McGuinness was born in Buncrana, County Donegal in 1953 and lectures in English at Maynooth University. His plays, which are remarkable for their theatrical innovation and imaginative exploration of language, have been performed widely at home and abroad. His greatest successes have been *The Factory Girls, Observe the Sons of Ulster Marching towards the Somme, Innocence, Carthaginians, Someone Who'll Watch Over Me* and *The Bird Sanctuary*. He has also adapted plays by Lorca, Ibsen, Chekhov, Brecht, Strindberg and Pirandello. In 1994 he published his first collection of poetry entitled *Booterstown* after the Dublin suburb where he lives.

Frank McGuinness, you live in a house surrounded by books and cats. Can you remember the first book you every bought?

The first book I ever paid money for was *Death of a Naturalist* by Seamus Heaney when I was about sixteen or seventeen. My mother was going to Derry and she came back cursing me because she spent half an hour going through the murder section of the SPCK Bookshop looking for this book, *Death of a Naturalist*. She finally found it and has come to like Seamus Heaney since then.

The first book I see here on your shelves is the World's Classics edition of Voltaire's 'Candide and Other Stories'.

It's a book that I particularly love and I've read it now about four times. I think it's one of the funniest books every written, also one of the wisest in its own satirical and very cynical way. Voltaire is a man who provokes many arguments so I definitely enjoy him.

I know from your lecturing in Maynooth that you are particularly enchanted by the poetry of John Keats and I see you have on your shelves a 'Penguin Literary Biography of Keats' by Robert Gittings.

Gittings' biography is probably the definitive work on Keats's life. One of my great interest in Keats is not just his achievements but what could have been achieved. He is someone I have been inspired by in many ways, not just because he had done so much so young but I do believe that when one reads his poetry and looks at the whole body of his work that the great missing dramatist in English is John Keats. The more I read of his later poetry in particular the more I think he was beginning to develop a very dramatic language. When one considers his early death and terrible suffering and how much he achieved, drama seems to me to be a very natural medium for him to be evolving into. He was moving from the lyrical voice into the dramatic voice and our great loss is that he never achieved that. There are few plays which are not particularly good but there are strong signs that here was a very great playwright in the making.

You have a lot of books on the theatre on your shelves and one of them is about life at London's Royal Court Theatre.

It's called *A Sense of Direction* and it is by one of the world's greatest theatre directors, William Gaskill. I love the way Gaskill writes because it is so free from pretension, so simple in its insights and so threatening in what it proposes a theatre should do. He is a man of very marked intelligence and as anyone who has seen his production knows, there is this wonderful analytic vein of comment being mined from the text and he matches that brilliant intelligence with a brilliant vision. He has a tremendous sense of what makes a play happen on stage. His essays in this book are a joy to read and it's always been a dream of mine that I would one day work with him. The book chronicles the wonderful heyday at the Royal Court in the '50s and '60s when they were not only producing the best of English theatre of the time but were also reinvesting in the classics and indeed European theatre with a vigour and a relevance to their world in much the same way as Michael Colgan is trying to do at the Gate Theatre in Dublin at the moment.

What are your favourite books on the theatre?

I think anything written by Peter Brook is always illuminating and I would also think that Stanislavsky's writings on the theatre gives a lot of food for thought – not much room for agreement but plenty to think about.

You have a novel by Irish writer Liam Lynch called 'Shell, Sea Shell' in pride of place on your shelves. Not a writer who is very well known.

I think Liam Lynch will become recognised in years to come. Liam is dead now but we met ten years ago at a workshop in Galway. Liam was already an established playwright and while we were there he mentioned this novel he was working on. At the time I had an association with Wolfhound Press and I asked him could I read it and along came this extraordinary book which was completely unique in my experience in Irish writing. It owed far more to the European tradition of the novel which never took root here, almost a visionary novel, a serious novel, not a novel that was going to employ comedy as a means of escape. It is written in three very distinct voices telling very separate stories but the subtleties of Lynch's writing is such that by the end of the book you are almost overwhelmed by the contingency of the various tragedies that have befallen these people and you end up feeling very darkly and very deeply for their fate. It is a great book and Liam Lynch is a great writer and the fact that he is not well known is the loss of the reading public.

Here's a bit of a surprise on your shelves. From the World's Classics series it's an edition of the Koran.

You'll see that I actually have a lot of bibles here and when I was working on *Observe the Sons of Ulster Marching Towards the Somme*, I read the whole Bible as my main research for it. The Koran is a book that I have been immersed in for some time as background to a play about hostages in Beirut called *Someone Who'll Watch Over Me*. I very deliberately did not want to put any actual Arab characters on stage but I wanted the text for the Koran to be almost a subtext to my play. The hostages in the play are given two books: the Koran and the Bible, and the Koran is quoted quite frequently in the course of the play and one of the recurring motifs is a verse from the Koran which is a warning against pride: 'Remember, over you there are watchers.' It is almost as if that is the line which gives the three hostages the spiritual sustenance to survive under the horrendous torture they are going through. I think that the great surprise of reading the Koran is to discover what a very tolerant religion the Muslim religion is and what a great beautiful faith it is as well. Like many from the Christian tradition I was not particularly well informed about the practical details of the Muslim religion and the Koran is an eye opener. That said, I think it might prove an eye opener to a lot of Muslims as well if they actually followed what it preaches.

Are there any books you went around hiding when you saw me coming with my tape recorder? Do you ever read trashy fiction, do you read detective fiction, do you read romance when you're not being high-minded and serious?

There would be a couple I'd hide from you, Seamus, because I know you'd want to borrow them! I don't read trashy novels too much but one weakness I have is that I love books about horse racing. It's my favourite sport. I'm not a great gambler but my grandfather was a gambler and one of the ways I learned to read was to read aloud the names of the horses for him. I like books on the history of horse racing and on contemporary racing as well. It is the one bit of light reading I might indulge in.

Here's a biography of Andy Warhol by Victor Bockris and it looks like it has been read and reread.

I think Andy Warhol is a fascinating character. If you grew up in the '60s as I did he is absolutely a key figure. He changed everything in the world of painting. He also changed a lot in the world of music and he gave the impetus to a whole generation to go out and do things and believe that they could do things. Having said that I think that he is a major figure by reason of his paintings. What people forget about Andy Warhol is that he was a very devout Greek Orthodox Catholic and he is steeped in the Orthodox faith. When he does these paintings of Campbell soup tins or contemporary figures like Mao Tse Tung or Marlyn Monroe he is giving to those portraits almost a saintly quality and he has invested the objects around us with the quality of the Russian icons. He is making something holy out of the ordinary and that is, I think, where his power and originality as a painter come from. He is tied very closely to a very ancient European tradition which he reinterprets in modern terms and that is where his significance lies. I'd put a gun to my head and say that Andy Warhol was as much a form of priest as he was a painter.

I know that as a playwright you have been hugely influenced by Shakespeare and what playwright could not be, and I see a very handsome edition of 'Shakespeare's Sonnets' published by the Royal Shakespeare Company in Stratford-on-Avon. Why do you keep coming back to the Sonnets of Shakespeare?

To me they are the keys to his plays. If one wants to understand the mind of the playwright and the operations of the playwright, look to the Sonnets. You'll never find out too much private about Shakespeare, nothing really private is known about him, but you can find out an awful lot about how his mind works from looking at the miniature dramas that are the Sonnets. We are all the time hoping that another play by Shakespeare will turn up but I think that the lost play is actually the Sonnets themselves. They are theatrical works, brilliant revelations of character and it is in the psychological unravelling of the Sonnets that you see the groundwork for the immensely complex more public characters of a Hamlet or a Lear or a Richard II. Everything that is elaborated on in those particular plays and in other plays can be found in miniature, in isolation in the Sonnets where the seeds were sown. They are also, of course, supremely glorious poetry and they bring peace when nothing else can. That's the most important book in my collection.

I suspect if the collection of Shakespeare's Sonnets is the most important book in your library, not far behind it comes 'The Selected Plays of Anton Chekhov' containing 'Uncle Vanya', 'Three Sisters', 'The Cherry Orchard' and 'The Wood Demon'. Why Chekhov?

It's the mood, the spirit he conjures up, the sense of being challenged when reading him. I had the privilege of doing a version of *Three Sisters* for the Cusack sisters and their father Cyril at the Gate Theatre. I've seen Patrick Mason's production of *The Cherry Orchard*. I know Tom Kilroy's version of *The Seagull* which he transposes to Ireland and Brian Friel's version of *Three Sisters* which is glorious and I've always wanted to know could I put myself against this man and try to uncover some of his wonderful secrets. He is a playwright who deals so much in the spilling of secrets, as Friel does, in particularising the moment when people talk and tell about their lives in a way that transforms their lives and indeed can transform the lives of an audience. It is these extraordinary moments which are collectively the plays of Chekhov and there is nobody who can write like him. He is a unique voice and it is that, in particular, which I look for in a playwright.

6

SEAMUS HEANEY

Seamus Heaney was born in County Derry and now divides his time between Dublin and Massachusetts where he is Boylston Professor of Rhetoric and Oratory at Harvard University. *Death of a Naturalist*, his first collection of poems, appeared in 1966, and since then he has published poetry, criticism and translations which have established him as one of the finest poets of the century. His eight collections of poetry include *Door Into the Dark*, *North*, *Fieldwork*, *Station Island*, *The Haw Lantern* and *Seeing Things*. He was Professor of Poetry at Oxford (1989 – 1994) and his Oxford Lectures, *The Redress of Poetry*, have just been published. His *New Selected Poems* appeared in 1990 and 1995 will see the publication of a new collection of poems *The Spirit Level*. In 1995 he was awarded the Nobel Prize for literature.

Seamus Heaney, for a man who lives by words, I'm not at all surprised to see a number of important and impressive looking dictionaries on your shelves including this thirteen volume 'Oxford Dictionary'.

That's a special one to me. First of all, because it is the thirteen volume *Oxford Dictionary in* thirteen volumes with a couple of supplements. There was a two volume edition of it put out with a magnifying glass a few years ago but I had this greed to get the whole thing. When I was resigning from Carysfort College in 1981 my colleagues gathered money for a presentation to me, asked me what I wanted and I said I would like the *Oxford Dictionary*. By coincidence, the librarian happened to be at the auctioning of the library of the Irish scholar David Greene and this is David Greene's thirteen volume *Oxford Dictionary*. I use it and it gives me great pleasure because of its lexical thoroughness and its historical magnificence, but also because it comes from the hands of a scholar as important and significant as Greene.

Dictionaries have a special place for me from Dinneen's *Irish–English Dictionary* which I still keep, not only for nostalgia's sake but because of the extraordinary riches of it, to *The English Dialect of Donegal* published by the Royal Hibernian Academy. This was a thesis really but for anybody from Northern Ireland it has a particular potency. Words themselves go right back into a primeval place in you, especially if that first place spoke a slightly different language. For example, there is the word 'colly' which means smut or coal dust and which we used at home. There's 'gunk' as in 'I got a bad gunk or fright' and 'gulpin' meaning an ignorant, unmannerly fellow. There's 'gully' meaning a large knife and 'gulder' meaning to shout or speak. You forget you knew them, then you open one of those pages and it's like a little trip back in time.

You have many versions of the classics – Homer, Dante, The Táin. What's that version of Homer's 'Odyssey'?

That's the version of the *Odyssey* that I read in the beginning. I had tried to read it in the old Penguin prose translation by E. V. Rieu but the first time I really got into it was in this version of Robert Fitzgerald who is American. He translated the *Iliad* and the *Odyssey* and this *Odyssey* was given to me when I was teaching at Queen's University by Eamon Carrigan who was then in the English Department. It is inscribed 'To help you with your water-borne tactician.' In this translation Odysseus, the man of many wiles, is called 'the great tactician' and he's always on the water. Later on, I got to know Robert Fitzgerald and wrote an introduction for this version of the *Odyssey* which has come out in the new Everyman series.

I've got different versions of Dante's *Inferno*. I got very, very interested in Dante in translation in the '70s. The least imposing-looking version is by Dorothy Sayers in the old Penguin edition. It's a real lolloping, galloping piece of *terza rima*. It's not great verse but it's in rhyme and it gives you a sense of the whole thing speeding along. I suppose the most impressive translation is this one by Singleton in six volumes, very scholarly with one volume of translation, then one volume of commentary for each of the three parts.

Here are two special volumes for you: Thomas Hardy's 'Wessex Poems' and his novel 'The Mayor of Casterbridge'. They both have a special significance for you?

They are part of a whole set and they are from the first bookshelf that I really was close to as a youngster, and then as an adolescent. My Aunt Sally as we called her, Sarah Heaney, was a schoolteacher in Ballyneese and in the front of this volume here is inscribed 'Sarah Heaney, October 1925'. As a young teacher she bought this complete set of Thomas Hardy's poems, novels and so on and that set of books sitting on a shelf in the house of one of my relations gave me a sense of books as a kind of precious thing in themselves. It looked lovely. Then Hardy happened to be the writer I got most out of when I was at school. I read *The Mayor of Casterbridge* and *The Woodlanders* in this edition, so it not only has the familial association but it also keeps alive my memories of the first reading of Hardy. Hardy was a wonderful poet and, of course, he stopped writing fiction in the 1890s and devoted himself for the rest of his life, until he died in 1928 at the age of 88, to writing poetry. His poetry at the very end is very plain, very wintery, very unpretentious and clear.

An early mentor of yours was Michael McLaverty and I see you have a very early edition of 'The Game Cock and Other Stories'.

You can see written on the inside leaf: 'To Seamus Heaney from Michael, 5 October 1965'. I hadn't published anything at that stage and Michael was the headmaster of the school where I was teaching. I think his short stories are actually small masterpieces. A number of his stories are completely true. The title story of this collection, *The Game Cock*, has a kind of melody and sureness and astuteness about people that makes it a perfect thing. In fact, John McGahern recognised the purity of McLaverty's genius early on. The kind of purity and reticence and devotion to the bare perfection of language itself that you find in McGahern's writing is also evident in McLaverty. McLaverty gave me a lot of books on these shelves when he was clearing out his own.

Here's a slim but very significant volume: 'The Complete Poems of Francis Ledwidge'.

It was edited by Lord Dunsany. Beside it is a book that meant a lot to me and still does. It's the biography of Francis Ledwidge by Alice Curtayne. Alice Curtayne usually did biographies of saints. She was a very good woman of letters. Her biography of Ledwidge gives a terrifically poignant view of the man from Slane, caught between the political currents of the time – between the Home Rule sense of Ireland where you have to go to the front and fight, and the new Sinn Féin sense where you have to stand off, break away. I like Ledwidge because of the pathos of the figure he cuts. The poems he wrote could be stronger but he himself as a person couldn't be.

You have many volumes of poetry on your shelves including this one by T. S. Eliot entitled 'The Collected Poems: 1909 – 1935'.

That particular volume of Eliot is the first serious book I owned myself. I was at St Columb's College in Derry, as a boarder and the college oddly enough like many boarding schools in Ireland in the 1940s and '50s was much devoted to putting its students through the academic hoop. But it had an oddly anti-intellectual attitude too. Books that weren't on your course and weren't in the library were suspect. Anyhow, when my aunt, who was manageress of a hotel in Rostrevor at the time, asked me what I would like for a present, I remember I ordered two books: *Tales of Mystery and Imagination* by Edgar Allen Poe and this *Collected Poems of T. S. Eliot*. I had to hide the Eliot in case it was found. It puzzled me and bewildered me at the time but there it is with '1955' written on the inside. Getting Eliot on my own initiative meant the beginning of aspirations at any rate.

Did that volume open the windows of wonder to you?

Well, no. To tell you the truth it opened a certain anxiety in the breast. I think the windows of wonder were opened by Hopkins in an old anthology, *A Pageant of English Verse,* which is up there among the anthologies. I had to wait until I left school, and almost until I had left university, until the writing excitement woke in me. I associate that with a whole other part of these bookshelves here such as *The Dolmen Miscellany of Irish Writing* which was put out by John Montague and Thomas Kinsella in the early 1960s. Richard Murphy gave me that volume. Then there were all the people writing in Ireland at that time: there was Patrick Kavanagh, who was very important and there's a whole set of books up there by him. Elizabeth Bishop is a poet of great purity and clarity. Her books have come to be specially precious to me because, among other things, I did know her and felt she didn't utterly disapprove of what I wrote. A lot of these books are important to me not only because of what they give to your memory, not only because of their impact on my imagination as texts, but because they are tokens of continuity and affection. Michael McLaverty, Elizabeth Bishop and Robert Fitzgerald – all of their books are resonant as imaginative products but the actual volumes are precious to me as much again because of the quality of the people who wrote them.

7

HUGH LEONARD

Hugh Leonard is the all-round man of letters – internationally acclaimed playwright, script writer for radio, television and cinema, iconoclastic newspaper columnist, writer of biography and autobiography, talk show pundit and witty panelist on RTE Radio's celebrity game show *Panel Beaters*. His most successful play internationally has been the autobiographical *Da*, a Tony Award Winner and now a film. Among his other theatre successes have been *The Poker Session*, *The Patrick Pearse Motel*, *A Life*, *Time Was* and *The Mask of Moriarty*. Two volumes of his autobiography have been published: *Home Before Night* and *Out After Dark*. He lives in Dalkey with his wife and a collection of celebrated cats.

Hugh Leonard, since you are a man of the theatre, I'm not at all surprised that the first volume I see here on your shelves is 'A Shorter Ego', the autobiography of James Agate. He's a man you admire?

In a sense I admire him but not as a theatre critic because he was so totally dishonest. He would go out and write a review under his own name and then write another under an assumed name and the two would be totally different. One would be hostile and one would like the play. He was a very strange man, a rather unpleasant man in many ways but he wrote like an angel. He had a most beautiful writing style and nobody could touch him for writing about great acting. He had a vast store of scholarship and could quote French references to the point of irritation. At one point in his life he started to write a kind of public diary, a celebration of what he called The Greater Truth, that is the truth that isn't true at all but sounds good. He did nine volumes of *Ego* and I managed to collect them all over the years, and after his death *A Shorter Ego* came out. This is a condensation of the nine volumes and it's wonderful beside reading. You can just soak in them forever. As a critic he was different to Kenneth Tynan. Someone said that Tynan didn't really love the theatre but he used it as a trampoline. He bounced up and down on it and used it as a springboard for his opinions and to get a position in the arts. I think that Agate, for his faults, was besotted by and absolutely in love with the theatre. Tynan is more fun to read. You can read his description of Anna Nagle in *The Glorious Years* shaking her voice at the audience 'like a tiny fist' and the conjecture going through the audience at the long interval on the opening night as to whether perhaps the star might not be hung up on a nail in the wings. Tynan was brilliant and wicked but Agate you read for style and information.

Given your own sense of humour and your love of the well turned phrase, it's no surprise to see you are a fan of P. G. Wodehouse. I see you have Benny Green's recent biography of Wodehouse.

I adore Wodehouse. Particularly everything he wrote between 1920 and 1950, his thirty-year peak. The Jeeves stories and particularly the Mr Mulliner stories were always my favourites. I remember my daughter and myself were sitting in the Algonquin Hotel in New York. We were watching a pianist and she was wondering what character in Wodehouse he reminded her of. He went over to talk to some people and we heard him say, 'Oh mercy, mercy, mercy', and Danielle burst out laughing and said 'Oh Dad, it's Gussie Fink Nottle'. Wodehouse brings people together. When you meet a lover or an admirer of Wodehouse there's a friendship already. At his best Wodehouse says exactly what he wishes to say. His descriptions of the guy tied to the rock 'waiting for the vulture to drop in for its lunch' or the aunt who had the expression on her face 'as if she had just caught the down express in the small of her back' are marvellous. His description of Jeeves clearing his throat like the noise 'of a sheep coughing on a far off hillside' and 'shimmering' into rooms is memorable. You can't touch Wodehouse: he never fades.

You have a Penguin Twentieth Century Classic 'Le Grand Meaulnes' by Alain Fournier well used.

I took it on holidays many years ago and thought I was going to hate it, but I read it and was entranced. It's the only book Fournier wrote – they've just found his body — he went missing in World War I in the trenches. He wrote this story about an outsize schoolboy who goes off on a kind of show-off mission into the woods and there he discovers a chateau and a ball and a girl who looks like a princess and a young boy who's in love with the girl. You think this is a fairytale and it has all the trappings of a fairytale until its conclusion when Meaulnes enters into tragedy. It is a brilliantly written short book. I've cherished the idea of adapting it for the theatre for a long time and I think I may con Michael Colgan into allowing me to put it on at the Gate Theatre.

Here's a rather large book entitled 'The Art of the Personal Essay: An Anthology from the Classical Era to the Present' selected by Philip Lopett.

I like essays. I like reading short pieces that are written for their own sake. This is a collection in which the first person singular plays a large part. In these personal essays the narrator is on the scene. Things are happening to him or he is doing things instead of being third person, cold dispassionate essays. I like to think of my column in the *Sunday Independent* as an essay or a lot of mini-essays stuck together. I bitterly regret the death of the essay because you can pick up J. B. Priestly's collection *Delight* in which he has fifty small essays on things which have delighted him and read it with great pleasure. Bernard Levin does it in a more flabby way. I think you have to be someone very well known in another field before your thoughts are worth putting into print.

You are a great fan of Somerset Maugham and you have here his 'Collected Short Stories'.

It is very rare that you see a human being in a state of transition but I remember we were taking off one Christmas for the West Indies. My daughter was about eleven when she put the familiar wail, 'Dad, have you anything to read?' I gave her Somerset Maugham's short stories: I had four volumes in Penguin. She read three volumes between Shannon and New York. She was only eleven but I could see that she had entered an entirely new world. They were her first really grown up stories and from there, there was no going back. I think Maugham is a wonderful storyteller. He can be dreadful in some of his novels but in his stories he covers an incredible span whether they are set in London or Malaya or China.

Another writer of short stories is L. A. G. Strong, a writer who is somewhat out of fashion now but I see his stories on your shelves.

I don't think he was ever in fashion. I think that was his problem. He was a schoolteacher for seven years before he ever published anything. This is the only book of his that ever won anything: it's *Thirty Selected Stories* and it won the Hawthornden Prize for Literature. Some of them are too short but he brings to life a time and a place that are unique. One of his stories is called 'The English Captain' and is set in the Public Baths in Dun Laoghaire. There is 'The Nice Bit of Stuff' which is about a clerk who marries a girl in his office. There are various comedy stories. One of the funniest stories every written is 'Mr Kerrigan and the Tinkers'. He ranges over a great many areas of Irish life and this volume is his monument.

Does the Irish short story in general appeal to you?

I had a great admiration for Frank O'Connor, but as Sean O'Faolain used to say O'Connor would rewrite his stories to a great extent and always to their detriment. O'Faolain and O'Connor didn't get on and Sean believed it was a form of forgery to rewrite your stories in the light of later maturity. If you read O'Connor's 'The Drunkard' in its two versions you will see that the first version is far superior. O'Faolain was a marvellous writer but he got caught between sex and religion and he didn't know where he was. He was terrified of sex and he was even more terrified of his religion and a lot of his stories were a kind of exorcism where he was trying to battle his way out of a kind of gut religion that wouldn't allow him to free himself in the moral sense.

You have an American published edition of 'The Journal of Arnold Bennett'.

Bennett was a journeyman writer and I often think I have a lot in common with him in the sense that he was a good man for the hard slog. One of my favourite novels is *The Old Wives' Tale* which I read on a boating holiday in France. I refused to do any work and I just sat in a corner and couldn't put the book down. Bennett lived a very interesting life at a time when the bookman was a feature of London life just as film stars are today. Bookmen were revered and toasted and they led a wonderful life. Bennett went to France and made himself fluent in French and became almost a Frenchman at one remove. He was buck-toothed and quite ugly and he was once heard to say, in Somerset Maugham's hearing, 'I am a nice man', and indeed he was but nobody ever gave him credit. He was always slightly a figure of fun but he wrote some damn good books.

We can't leave your bookshelves without mentioning a Russian Classic. You have The Folio Society Edition of Leo Tolstoy's novel 'Anna Karenin'.

She is my darling. I have a Penguin edition for taking away on holidays. I was on an island in the Grenadines and there had nothing to read until I found *Anna Karenin*. I found it as easy to read as Harold Robbins but infinitely superior of course. A wonderful book, very very simply written, an engrossing narrative which I read in two days and then went home, started it again and read it properly. I always thought from the Garbo film that Anna Karenin was a tragic heroine and it is Tolstoy's fault for calling the book after her. She is nothing of the sort. She is a ninny. She goes rushing off giving everything away for the sake of an infatuation whereas Kitty, who marries the man Anna jilts, is the real heroine and lives a life of usefulness and enjoys a very nice relationship. Tolstoy is a writer I come back to time and again, a writer I cherish more as I get older.

8

PATRICK MASON

Patrick Mason is Artistic Director of the Abbey Theatre. He first joined the Abbey in 1977 as a theatre director and for twenty years has been responsible for some of the National Theatre's greatest successes at home and abroad. Among his most memorable productions for the Abbey Theatre are *You Never Can Tell*, *The Winter's Tale*, *The Cherry Orchard*, *Talbot's Box*, *The Gigli Concert*, and six MacIntyre works including *The Great Hunger* which was seen in Belfast, London, Paris, Leningrad, Moscow, Philadelphia and New York. His greatest international success as a director came with Brian Friel's *Dancing at Lughnasa* which transferred to the West End and later played Broadway where he won a Tony Award for Best Director in 1992. He has also directed theatre in Britain and the United States.

Patrick Mason, you're a great reader of poetry and the first volume I see on your shelves is Thom Gunn's recent collection 'The Man With Night Sweats'.

It's actually a collection that was given to me by Frank McGuinness who is a great pointer of people in the right direction in terms of poetry and literature. I have always admired Thom Gunn's work and this has become one of my favourite collections. It is steely and tender all at the same time. His work is generally clear and lucid but this collection is set apart because there is this deep emotion, this extraordinary grief for the appaling kind of decimation the AIDS epidemic has caused in San Francisco. These are very moving poems, very simple and direct but they have wit as well as irony. They are not at all sentimental. The collection is about an honesty in the face of this extraordinary tragedy. There is one particularly fine poem called 'The Reassurance'.

About ten days or so
After we saw you dead
You came back in a dream.
I'm all right now you said.

And it was you, although
You were fleshed out again;
You hugged us all round then,
And gave your welcoming beam.

How like you to be kind,
Seeking to reassure.
And, yes, how like my mind
To make itself secure.

You worked a lot with Tom MacIntyre and I see his collection of poetry here. It's called 'A Glance Will Tell You And A Dream Confirm' and it's published by Daedalus Press. You've had an extraordinary working relationship with Tom MacIntyre over the years.

Yes, it's a relationship that started a long time ago. I'd just arrived in the Abbey Theatre as a director in the mid '70s when Tomas Mac Anna handed me an extraordinary script called *Jack Be Nimble* and said, 'Now, you're to go off and meet this man.' I said, 'Fine, now where do I meet him?' 'Inishboffin,' he said. So I set off for the island and there on the quay to meet me was this extraordinary figure with flowing beard and hair. I spent a week on Inishboffin working on the script with him. Then in the '80s we collaborated on a whole series of plays with Tom Hickey including *The Great Hunger* and *Rise Up Lovely Sweeney* and most recently *Sheep's Milk On the Boil.* He is the most extraordinary individual voice in the Irish theatre. I think he is radical and he is always dangerous; sometimes it succeeds, sometimes it fails, but there's always excitement. Although in the theatre he is associated with imagery and visual gestural style I find his use of language extraordinarily powerful – lyrical, beautiful, haunting. This collection of poetry is full of very condensed, haunting, imagistic poems, very finely wrought and very musical. There's one I particularly like called 'Hoof-Taps'.

Banished for years
the horse opens
my door again,

and I'm afraid,
fear those hooves,
fear that fecund breath

while, insouciantly
as an old lover,
he makes bold, fondles
me to recognition
of pure betrothal –

Say your prayers
by the West Gate;
drink, savour;
turn your face
to the Gates of The Sea.

Another writer who, like MacIntyre, is exuberant in his language as he was in his life, is Anthony Burgess and I see you have 'A Dead Man in Deptford' here on your shelves.

I think it's one of his last novels and by his standards one of his shortest, most condensed. It tells the extraordinary story of Christopher Marlowe, the Elizabethan playwright, who was famously, or infamously, murdered in an inn in Deptford and his involvement in the Elizabethan Secret Service of the time as a spy for the government tracking down recusant priests and involved in the whole plot to undermine Queen Elizabeth I by crowning Mary, Queen of Scots. Exuberant is hardly the word: his language is extraordinary and it's a celebration of the richness of Elizabethan English and its roots in Latin. It has that intoxicating feel that is so much in Marlowe and in Shakespeare, the forging of a new language. They were just making language and there's this rich abandon to the whole thing. It's a great read because it's a fantastic story and Burgess tells it wonderfully well. It's a spy thriller full of political manoeuvring and incredibly rich characters.

His observation of the smells and sights and sounds of Elizabethan London are very perceptive and the wittiest thing in the novel is the strange figure whom you keep glimpsing but who is only a minor character in the whole scheme of things. This is, of course, Will Shakespeare. It's a nice trick because he keeps coming closer but he keeps going out of shot again. It's a great read, very exciting, very vivid and deftly told.

You are a great admirer of the poet Seamus Heaney, and I see his 1986 'T. S. Eliot Memorial Lectures, The Government of the Tongue', on your shelves.

Seamus Heaney is one of my favourite poets but also I find that his other writing, the critical essays, so stimulating. His prose style is so clean, so clear. I am desperately envious of it whenever I have to write documents and essays and backgrounds to plays. I have such a struggle with the word processor it's unbelievable. Words don't seem to do what I want them to do and then I read such wonderfully poised prose as Heaney's. It's such a pleasure to sense this wonderful clear mind, incisive and inspiring. The great thing about the essay is the extraordinary clarity of thought and things said in a sense that you've always known it but you've never been able to express it and suddenly it all makes sense or suddenly a new perspective opens up. In a similar vein, Ted Hughes, again a great poet, in *Winter Pollen*, a collection of his occasional prose, gives us a book to go back to time and time again. There's a wide range of topics dealt with and always fascinating insights and arresting phrases.

Here's an interesting, if somewhat esoteric volume. It's 'Eleusis: Archetypal Image of Mother and Daughter' by Manheim Kerenyi.

Well, Kerenyi was a great mythologist, a collector of odd myths. In fact, he worked very closely with Carl Jung, the Swiss psychologist, collaborating on several papers. He has produced a series of books on the Greek myths in particular and the figure of the gods and goddesses. This is a book on Eleusis which was the site of the great mysteries of the ancient world, one of the greatest and longest running religious mysteries of the ancient world. The thing about the Eleusian mysteries, as Brian Friel so memorably pointed out in *Wonderful Tennessee*, is that actually they are mysteries and no one ever reveals what went on. We know there was some extraordinary revelation and you have the evidence of people like Sophocles saying, 'Happy the man who has seen the mysteries of Eleusis because he has no fear of death'. They had an extraordinary influence and we know very little. What Kerenyi has done is through archaeology, and through myth and historical fragments he has put together a very convincing description of what may have occurred at Eleusis and what that extraordinary moment might have been. You can't understand anything about the ancient world if you don't look at Eleusis. It's centred around the myth of Demeter and Persephone, the great Earth Mother. I always have had an interest in myth and the writings of Jung and in the whole question of the nature of archetype and how these extraordinary stories and figures come to us and shift and change and yet seem to resonate from age to age. Kerenyi is one of the best collectors of myths and one of the best writers on this. Yes, it's maybe esoteric but it's like a kind of private obsession for me. It keeps me going!

You mentioned Brian Friel in passing there and it's no surprise to see his Collected Plays have pride of place on your shelves.

I've known Brian Friel and admired his work for a very long time but I'd never actually worked on one of his plays until we did *Dancing at Lughnasa* and it obviously was a great opportunity and a tremendous pleasure to work on that play. Then to follow that up with *Wonderful Tennessee* which I still believe to be one of the most remarkable plays, which at the time caused a great division of opinion, was a wonderful privilege. The sheer mastery of that play and its extraordinary power for me and for many people, the range, the intensity, the achievement is without question absolutely world class. Just recently we had the wonderful *Molly Sweeney* and that was such a pleasure to see. He is a very influential playwright and any of his texts have this extraordinary music to them and you cannot do these plays unless you acknowledge that. They are extremely demanding texts, but the rewards for writing with Friel make the challenge and the difficulties infinitely repaid.

9

RICHARD MURPHY

Richard Murphy, one of Ireland's most accomplished poets, was born in County Galway to a Protestant family. He spent part of his childhood in Ceylon and was educated at public schools in England and at Oxford. He has lectured extensively on poetry and literature and has read his poetry all over the world. Among his most acclaimed collections of poetry are *Sailing to an Island* (1963), *The Battle of Aughrim* (1968), *High Island* (1974) and his *New Selected Poems* (1985) which includes Murphy's sequences *Care* and *The Price of Stone*. After moving to Dublin from the west of Ireland he now lives at Knockbrack on Killiney Hill with a picturesque view of Dublin Bay.

We're in Mullin's Hill, just up from Killiney in County Dublin in the sitting room of poet Richard Murphy, a room that is crowded with books. Is there one book of all you possess which means something special in your life?

I think by far the most important book in my life is the Bible given to me on my seventh birthday by my mother and father. You can see the inscription here: she wrote it herself, perhaps that's why the inscription reads: 'With love from his mother and father'. Mother comes first. This Bible was so sacred a book I could never put any other book on top of it, nor a candle nor a box of matches. That would have been sacrilegious. To this day I wouldn't let you put a book on it now. I think that this Bible which is bound in Moroccan leather has illustrations which I loved when I was a child but are quite horrendously vulgar. It was the Society for the Promoting of Christian Knowledge that published it. It is the King James version and I used to read it by candlelight at Milford, the house where I was born. Then there's another Bible which was given to me on 28 July 1938 on my admission as a singing boy at Canterbury Cathedral and that was the one I read mostly thereafter. On 23 March 1940, just before the Germans' Panzer Division tore through Belgium and into France and we were evacuated from Canterbury I was presented with a beautiful blue leather Bible on my admission as a chorister of Canterbury Cathedral. That was such a good book I never opened it, never dared to read it in case I damaged it. In 1977 I was a visiting professor at Syracuse University and I decided I wanted to read the King James version of the Bible so why not give a course on the Poetry of the King James Bible? I read it from cover to cover. In the past I read the Bible with tremendous awe and my reading of the Bible influenced all my reading. I read everything with far too much awe: I was always on my knees before the text and generally tended to imagine that there was something wrong with me if I didn't agree with what the Bible said. In fact, all books became either sacred or sacrilegious because of the Bible. Because of their relationship to it they were either divine or satanic. This, I think, raised and enhanced the importance of literature in my mind on the unconscious level. Then in 1977 reading the Bible from cover to cover as a work of literature I was amazed at the extraordinary skill with which the Hebrew rhetoricians managed to overcome the reader and convince the reader that every word they had written had been uttered by God. So powerful is the text of thousands of years ago that it has altered the map of the Middle East today. That's the power of the Bible.

What about novels – did they influence your imaginative life as a child?

When I was about eleven or twelve years old, just before the war, at home in County Mayo on holiday from Canterbury Cathedral Choir School, early in the morning I used to go into my mother's bedroom and get in to her bed. One morning I noticed that she was reading a novel which she didn't really want me to read and she covered her face with the book. Of course, I was very interested as to what could absorb my mother's attention to the extent that she didn't want my kisses or hugs any more. The novel was called *Kenilworth* by Sir Walter Scott and I said I'd love to read it but of course it was way above my head. The following term at Canterbury she visited me and she had a brand new copy to give me as a present in the Nelson's Classics series. I read it from cover to cover feeling I must not miss a single work, it was so important. Partly out of pride because everything we did in that wretched boy's boarding school was done out of competition. I had to keep up with and keep ahead of

William Maine who was a contemporary of mine. Reading Scott put me far ahead for that particular moment. But I did enjoy it. It's about the Earl of Leicester and the murder of his wife Amy whom he wanted to get rid of by throwing her down the stone stairs at Kenilworth Castle because he wanted to marry Queen Elizabeth I.

I see a lovely little edition here of Maria Edgeworth's 'Tour in Connemara and the Martyns of Ballinahinch' published by Constable in 1950.

This is special because it was given to me to review by the Literary Editor of *The Spectator*. I was enthralled by it because it took me back to Connemara which I was missing when I was in London. Maria Edgeworth undertook this tour of Connemara before the Famine and it was written in the form of a letter to her brother Packenham Edgeworth who was in India in the East Indies Service. It's a wonderful account of one of those great Anglo-Irish houses in decline. The Martyns went bankrupt during the Famine because they couldn't and didn't collect rents although they had to pay their rates.

You've always had a great interest in Oriental literature and I see you have a fine two-volume edition of 'The Tales of Genji'.

This medieval novel is a fascinating account of Japanese court life written by a woman, Lady Murusaki, a lady of the Emperor's Court in the twelfth century. It's a classic of Japanese literature and can stand with the great masterpieces of world literature. It's the account of Prince Genji who is the most outrageously promiscuous man you can imagine, written from the woman's point of view.

You've been a great admirer of Thomas Hardy and you have here a well thumbed copy of his Complete Poems.

Yes, Hardy is what Philip Larkin called an antidote to the Celtic Twilight of Yeats. I love Hardy but, of course, I loved Yeats long before I became acquainted with Hardy. I couldn't read Hardy in my twenties and thirties. I think I was forty before I really got interested in his poetry. Of course,

Hardy's best poetry was written in his later years. His language tended to be regarded as quaint. T. S. Eliot hadn't thought much of him and the modernists had rather pushed him to one side and his use of rare words made him seem too rural. He had an extraordinary facility for rhyme.

The Stories of Anton Chekhov I see in various editions on your shelves.

I read Chekhov now, not the way I read the Bible, but with as much respect. Every sentence Chekhov writes you can test for its truth against your senses first, your reason and also your imagination. The truth of his writing is what really comes home and the heart at the back of it all. You know he went to Ceylon and he wrote to his brother, 'Take your trousers in your mouth and choke yourself with envy that I am in Ceylon'. He had a wonderful sense of exuberance and also he is particularly known for his understatement, which is why I was so appalled by Michael Bogdanov's Dublin production of *The Cherry Orchard* in which he had a chainsaw starting up when Firs comes in at the very end and a wretched tree comes through the big high wall at the back of the stage, making an almighty noise. It was the sort of noise that Chekhov denounced when Stanislavsky tried to make noises in the theatre. Total un-Chekhovian production where the director tried to have the last word. Nothing to do with the truth at all. Firs (Cyril Cusack) sat down an emancipated slave who didn't want to be emancipated! He sits down in the very final moment of the play for the first time when everybody else is gone but that was lost in that production because Cyril Cusack as Firs was chatting as if he was the squire.

Among your contemporaries I see the work of John McGahern very prominent in your collection – 'The Dark', 'The Barracks', 'Amongst Women'.

A wonderful writer. I have the highest respect for him. His are amongst my favourite books, ones that have really influenced me and John would agree with me that Chekhov is the master. We can all learn so much from him.

10

GEMMA HUSSEY

As a member of the Fine Gael Party Gemma Hussey served at several levels in Irish political life – as Senator, Dáil Deputy, Cabinet Minister and member of the Council of State. Having obtained a degree in Economics and Political Science she worked in business and then became a spokesperson for the Irish women's movement before entering politics. Since retiring from politics she has published *At the Cutting Edge: Cabinet Diaries, 1982–87* and *Ireland Today: Anatomy of a Changing State*. She is a regular broadcaster and contributor to the debate on Ireland's political, social and cultural life.

Gemma Hussey, given your career in politics, I'm not at all surprised that the first book that catches my eye on your bookshelves is 'The Boss: Charles J. Haughey in Government' by Joe Joyce and Peter Murtagh. How far does this book go towards capturing the essence of this enigmatic politician?

It does capture him. It is amazing because I think it was the first serious political book in modern Irish political life. I know that's a sweeping statement but it describes the period of government of Charles Haughey from February to November 1982 and that coincided with my first six months in the Dáil as well. I distinctly remember that period and the tensions and the drama and never knowing what was going to happen next. It was the GUBU period as Conor Cruise O'Brien called it. This book came out, and to tell you the truth, we all waited for seventeen different libel actions to be slapped against everybody in sight but nothing transpired. It was quite brave of Poolbeg Press and the authors to go ahead with it. It is a remarkable and most entertaining book, and with Mr Haughey now retired, it gives you a perspective on what Irish political life was like in the early 1980s. It was a jungle to be pitched into; we had three elections one after another and I was a candidate in all three. It was like a roller coaster. You were up one day and down the next and the government kept falling so you were back out on the hustings. Then there was this uneasy six month period when Mr Haughey could not have anticipated what was going to happen including incidents like the McArthur murder. At the end of that period the era of my innocence was over and I was pitched into government. It's a great book, a great read.

A book that represents the other side of the political fence is 'Belling the Cats: Selected Speeches and Articles of John Kelly'. He was the great phrase-maker and coiner of memorable and colourful descriptions in Irish politics. Is that why his writings appeal to you?

John Kelly, who is such a terrible loss to Irish Politics, was the master of the phrase. I remember at a parliamentary party meeting in my early days in politics John got up and he lambasted all round him at some hypocrisy. In the course of doing that he was never unkind or personal. He never said an unkind or cruel word to anybody or about anybody. He usually managed to throw in a joke into what he was saying. A new senator who had come up from an area in rural Ireland said to me after that meeting, 'I would have paid in to hear that!'

John wouldn't speak in the Dáil too often but any time he signalled that he wanted to speak the whips would always make way for him because we knew that he had something to say and that it would be said in a thoughtful way and, if possible, a non-party way. There were a great many qualities to John Kelly, not least of which was his sense of humour.

On his feet making speeches, he was sparkling and you never knew what was going to come out. Just opening the book almost at random gives us an example of his wit. He was a great defender of all politicians. He felt that they were a much maligned group of people and he also thought that a lot of it was their own fault. However, he did defend politicians. Here he's making a speech on 3 November 1983 in the Dáil. Apparently people had been criticising TDs for going off on long holidays in the summer and he says:

> The vulgarity and ignorance of this point of view about deputies is, I'm sorry to say, not corrected by the press. We've all seen cartoons of a couple of deputies, their facial characteristics about as hateful as could be contrived within

the parameters of what is possible in a Hibernian countenance. On the beach, on the Costa Brava with their trouser bottoms rolled up paddling in the wavelets and their suitcases behind them marked TD with some cynical remark passing from one to the other about it being 'great to have three months of this ahead of us, Mick'.

John Kelly goes on in this comic vein and the book of his speeches and writings edited by John Fanigan is a great read.

Anybody trying to understand complexities of contemporary Ireland could probably do no better than to read this next book: 'J. J. Lee's Ireland 1912–1985: Politics and Society'. That, I would say, is a book that is dear to your heart.

I don't know how anybody could possibly live in modern Ireland without reading J. J. Lee or indeed reading another very fine book by Roy Foster on contemporary Irish history. Lee does something in this book which is not normally done in history books. He gives the history of the country with a great many very strong personal slants but the wonder of the research is amazing. When I admire this book I admire it for its scholarship, for a wonderful refreshing language, for a new understanding on very many aspects of Irish history. I wouldn't be entirely a subscriber to the rather pessimistic view of Ireland that J. J. Lee seems to bring forward. He stops in 1985 which was maybe a depressed time. I think there is a lot more hope around now even though unemployment is so high. It is a great book and I think everybody should keep it by their bedside and no matter where you open it you'll find some new look at what you thought about Irish history.

Another slant on Irish history and indeed on contemporary Ireland can be found in the next two books on your shelves which are Paul Durcan's collections of poetry 'Going Home to Russia' and 'Daddy, Daddy'.

I'm not given to reading poetry normally: I have dipped extensively into Seamus Heaney but I could not be described as that knowledgeable about poetry. I admire very much Patrick Kavanagh's 'The Great Hunger'. But Paul Durcan seems to combine very acerbic social commentary with terribly emotionally gripping poetry. In many ways he gives the impression of somebody who is tortured and who sees everything in a most dramatic light. Some of it is terribly funny, some of it is terribly sad, some of it is almost blasphemous you might feel, but it's fantastic. Almost at random opening his collection *Daddy, Daddy* I find a little poem picked almost out of nowhere. It's called 'Felicity in Turin'.

> We met in the Valentino in Turin
> And travelled down through Italy by train,
> Sleeping together.
> I do not mean having sex.
> I mean sleeping together.
> Of which sexuality is,
> And is not, a part.
> It is this sleeping together
> That is sacred to me.
> This yawning together.
> You can have sex with anyone
> But with whom can you sleep?
>
> I hate you
> Because having slept with me
> You left me.

I see from looking at your shelves that you're a great reader of fiction also. You have Ben Kiely's novel 'Proxopera' prominently among contemporary Irish fiction.

I think this was the first Ben Kiely that I read. The dedication, in many respects, speaks volumes about this little book. It is dedicated 'In memory of the innocent dead'. It's a slim volume, a beautifully and gently written story of a man in his late sixties, early seventies, who comes home from holidays in Donegal to his home in the North of Ireland. He returns with his son, his daughter-in-law and two grandchildren. He discovers the IRA have taken over his house. They make him get into a van to take a proxy bomb somewhere. Proxy bombs as a concept in the 1970s were even more horrific because it was a concept that was new to us. There is no blood and violence in the story. It's a gently told story and all the more striking for that. It's full of love and compassion and a strong bitter hatred of men of violence. It's a beautiful book and a great help to understanding Northern Ireland.

Another novel by an Irish writer I see is J. G. Farrell's 'The Singapore Grip'. He wrote very well about that part of the world.

Yes – he also wrote *The Siege of Krishnapur* and of course *Troubles* set in Ireland and made into a television series. I met Jimmy Farrell once and he was a lovely, gentle person who was drowned tragically in County Cork. He had polio when he was a child and wasn't able to help himself when he got swept into the sea by a wave. *The Singapore Grip* is an astonishingly broad and rich tapestry of Singapore just before the Japanese invaded and the details of the lives of the British and all those people with everything crumbling about their ears. It's a big book written with a gentle humour and great compassion. He would have written such amazing works had he lived longer.

You have a biography of Elizabeth Barrett Browning, English poet and critic, by Margaret Forster which you think is a model of literary biography.

I love biography and, to use the old cliché, this I could not put down. It gives you extraordinary insights into Elizabeth Barrett Browning. The interesting thing is that the author, Margaret Forster, also wrote a book called *Lady's Maid* about the maid who served Elizabeth Barrett Browning. To read those two books together gives you the feeling that writing could never be the same again. Elizabeth Barrett Browning, an amazing genius; was much stronger than we all thought she was and Margaret Forster is, in my view, one of greatest biographers writing today.

11

ROSALEEN LINEHAN

Rosaleen Linehan is Ireland's most versatile actress having played comedy, tragedy, musicals, revue, solo performances on radio, television, cinema and theatre. With her partner, Des Keogh, she kept the nation laughing in a series of theatre revues and radio comedy programmes scripted by her husband, Fergus Linehan. Among her most memorable roles in the theatre are Madam Arcati in *Blithe Spirit*, Feste in *Twelfth Night*, Mrs Malaprop in *The Rivals*, Bessie Burgess in *The Plough and the Stars*, Madge in *Philadelphia Here I Come* and Kate in *Dancing at Lughnasa* which she played in Dublin, London and New York. She starred in the musical *Mary Makebelieve* which she co-wrote with her husband Fergus and created the memorable role of Kathleen Behan in her solo show *Mother of All the Behans* which played at home and abroad, most recently Off-Broadway in the Autumn of 1994.

We're in Rosaleen Linehan's book-lined study in her home in the leafy Dublin suburb of Blackrock. Have you gone through phases in your reading over the years?

Phases would probably be too important a word to use. Until I was about eleven I was a voracious reader and had got as far as the Brontës and *Gone with the Wind* and some Denis Wheatley from a rather racy neighbour who was two years younger than me. Then at about the age of eleven or twelve the Irish education system at the time unfortunately took over my life and reading was not incorporated into that educational system at all. So I really stopped reading at about twelve which was a great pity. My external life was taken up with two subjects which were outside the curriculum: music and art. They took up any leisure time I had. I read the odd magazine over those years and then I did the dastardly thing of studying economics in University College Dublin which meant that I didn't really read then either and I was scattered around looking at fellas and going to dances. Then I got married and there was no time at all to

read. This means that there is a missing block of about twenty years in my reading life. When you have small children the most you'll find yourself opening is *Woman's Own* as the light is about to go out to see what your stars say for next week. ·

You mention music and, of course, music has played a very important part in your life. You have written for the musical theatre, you've performed on the musical stage and I see here on your shelves two collections of songs. One is 'A Family Song Book' and the other is 'Songs of the Irish' by O'Sullivan.

They are prominent on the shelves because I love them and I love songs and I love the piano. *Moore's Melodies* is another favourite. I get huge pleasure from song books. I also have all the lyrics of Cole Porter and Rodgers and Hart. I have the scores of *Oklahoma* and *Guys and Dolls* and the words of Sondheim's *Sweeney Todd* because the accompaniment is too difficult.

Are there shades of Victorian evenings around the piano in the Linehan household?

No, but there was in the McMenamin household where I grew up. My mother was a great enthusiast and played the piano well. We used to stand around the piano and sing. Musical evenings are very much part of Christmas, birthdays and special occasions like that.

A singer and a character you captured for ever was Kathleen Behan, and I see a well thumbed copy of 'Mother of All the Behans' on your shelves.

I was completely attracted to Kathleen Behan before I ever read this book through listening to her songs. I had gone up to Annaghmakerrig two months before the idea for the show was mooted and one of the records I brought with me for relaxation was Kathleen Behan Sings, a record which was made when she was ninety-two. The wonder of hearing her sing was marvellous; with no lyrics in front of her she could sing dozens of songs from memory. She was like a ballad singer. She sang straight through from the head to the voice. She didn't do any dressing of a song:

she just sang it. I came back from Annaghmakerrig and I received a phone call from the Abbey Theatre to go in and discuss a project and that was to become the show *Mother of All the Behans* directed by Peter Sheridan. The theatre is full of coincidences like that and, of course, I took in this great enthusiasm for Kathleen Behan with me.

You are also a great fan of poetry and I see 'The Collected Poems of Philip Larkin'. What appeals to you about Larkin?

Manic depressive! Every comic is a manic depressive, the other side of the clown. Seriously though, I think they are wonderful poems. I am a terrible didactic person as my children and fellow workers will tell you. There is an awful lot of the school-marm in me but that works two ways. I have this voracious desire to learn and I write down pieces out of books I've read that will see me through, something that I'll take on. In Philip Larkin I find wonders because I'm such a flashy actress. I see that as one of my difficulties and I'm sure my directors do too. I write things into my diary that I think are wise. I have one quotation here from *My Life in the Theatre* by Tyrone Guthrie, who is one of my gods.

> I believe that a theatre where live actors perform to an audience which is there in the flesh before them will survive all threats from powerfully organised industries which pump prefabricated drama out of cans and blowers and contraptions of one kind or another. The struggle for survival may often be hard and will batter the old theatre about severely. Indeed, from time to time it will hardly be recognisable but it will survive as long as mankind demands to be amused, terrified, shocked, instructed, corrupted and delighted by tales told in a manner which will always remain mankind's most vivid and powerful manner of telling a story.

Through a life of living in the theatre we all know that's what happens. There are times when you think it's never going to rise again and then suddenly somebody comes through, especially, thank God in this country, where the writer is alive and kicking. The same thing happens in your life as an actor. Sometimes you get tired of the theatre and then a part comes along you can't resist. I have Richard Brindsley Sheridan's play *The Rivals* on the go at the moment even though I swore I'd never work at Christmas again. Mrs Malaprop is such a wonderful character really. I even put in a few malapropisms of my own like, 'I cannot control my ejaculations!' I hope Sheridan won't mind.

Other theatre books here on your shelves include the writings of Artaud.

That's much more arty Artaud than my view of the theatre usually is but I got so excited when I read Artaud on the theatre that my hair was standing on end and I felt that if I was seventeen again this is where I would go now. Even much later I would try to incorporate a lot of what that man said the theatre should be about and what the relationship between theatre and an audience should be. I sometimes get desperately excited when reading a book and that was one of them even though Artaud writes about the kind of theatre I'm not really involved in. It's off the side. I'm much more mainstream and much more in the commercial theatre so I'm very aware of what an audience likes. I hope I don't try to please them too much but I hope from time to time I do.

Another book about the theatre, or rather about theatres, is 'The Great Theatres of London' by Ronald Bergin.

This is something to do with my lack of a sense of direction. I don't know whether to turn left or right and particularly in the West End of London. I remember a theatre from the shows that play in it. It took me about six weeks in London to find the theatre even when I was playing in it! I'd have to set out an hour beforehand so that I could find it. The National Theatre in London was no problem because unless you fell into the Thames you turned into the National. But once you got inside the National there was another problem because it's like a maze inside. Apparently, elderly actors like Ralph Richardson used to wander on to the wrong stage. It really is like a huge civil service building.

You have 'The Collected Poems of Louis MacNeice' here and he seems to be a favourite of yours.

I see I gave this to my husband Fergus in 1979, one of those mean things I did because I wanted to read it myself. I love MacNeice's long poem *Autumn Journal* and some passages I come back to again and again, like this one.

> Why do we like being Irish? Partly because
> It gives us a hold on the sentimental English
> As members of a world that never was,
> Baptised with fairy water;
> And partly because Ireland is small enough
> To be still thought of with a family feeling,
> And because the waves are rough
> That split her from a more commercial culture;
> And because one feels that here at least one can
> Do local work which is not at the world's mercy
> And that on this tiny stage with luck a man
> Might see the end of one particular action.
> It is self-deception of course;
> There is no immunity in this island either;
> A cart that is drawn by somebody else's horse
> And carrying goods to somebody else's market.

He has a very black moment later in the same poem when he says:

> Why should I want to go back
> To you, Ireland, my Ireland?
> The blots on the page are so black
> That they cannot be covered with shamrock.

It is very bleak, although he did say later in his life that he did not really find it so. Looking back, maybe he did not really mean it to sound as harsh. But it still does mean a lot even today.

One last book?

I try to avoid theatre criticism except if it is Kenneth Tynan. Here's James Agee in 1944 talking about the young Elizabeth Taylor in the film *National Velvet*.

> Frankly I doubt if I am qualified to arrive at any sensible assessment of Miss Taylor. Ever since I first saw the child two or three years in, I forget what minor role in what movie, I have been choked with the particular sort of adoration I might have felt if we were both in the same grade of primary school.

He goes on to say he does not know how her career will develop but he feels it will be quite extraordinary. He sure got it right.

12

BENEDICT KIELY

Benedict Kiely is a native of County Tyrone but he has lived most of his life in Dublin. He is a celebrated writer of novels and short stories, a biographer, *Irish Press* journalist and a distinguished broadcaster famous for his colourful contributions to *Sunday Miscellany* on RTE Radio. Among his best known works are the collections of short stories – *A Journey to the Seven Streams, Dogs Enjoy the Morning* and *A Ball of Malt and Madame Butterfly* – and the novels *The Cards of the Gambler, Proxopera* and *Nothing Happens in Carmincross*. He has published a celebration of Ireland, *All the Way to Bantry Bay*, a memoir, *Drink to the Bird* and *Poor Scholar: A Life of William Carleton.*

Ben Kiely, when we stand in front of your well-stocked bookshelves looking at your vast collection of books it must be like a trip down memory lane for you because so many of the authors represented here are, or were, your friends.

This is true, because over the years I did meet very many people and since I was in the newspaper business I did encounter an awful lot of writers. (An awful lot sounds wrong but quite a lot of writers.) Then there are other books that were not written by friends but were associated with them. When you look at those books you remember friends.

Such a book is *Stone Mad* by Seamus Murphy, a great craftsman and a great writer. He was a man of infinite good humour, a most extraordinary man. I met him first in Dublin but to visit him in his native Cork added something completely new to that city. As a sculptor he knew every stone everywhere by name and he could nearly draw you a map of Ireland charting stone locations. In fact it's in that book *Stone Mad* that he talks about the old stone cutters and how they measured the country by the nature of the stone here and there. That was their map. He was like that himself – he was so devoted to stone being a great sculptor and having known the old stone cutters. Stone was his life. The old stonies, as he called them, were the same. Seamus Murphy picked that up and elaborated on it and the whole book he wrote is filled with his devotion to stone and his knowledge of it. He knew localities by the nature of the stone that came out of them.

No surprise to see on your shelves that comic masterpiece by your fellow Tyrone man, Flann O'Brien's 'At Swim-Two-Birds'.

You see both our mothers were Gormley so we were probably ninety-second cousins. Brian O'Nolan or Flann O'Brien was a most extraordinary man. He had a name for being a bit irascible but I never found him so. I thought him thoroughly entertaining and tremendously informative. He knew an enormous amount and you can see that the whole technique of the book shows that. He was an extremely scholarly man, most learned. It comes out in this extraordinary novel. In and around University College Dublin that novel was an earth-shaker when it first came out because there were scenes that derived from UCD and the character of the place was reflected in it. It had a tremendous influence on students of my time, and for a long time afterwards. It was a sort of Bible and men like Martin Sheridan and Tommy Woods could quote it ad lib.

The great Donegal novelist Patrick McGill is represented on your shelves by 'Children of the Dead End'.

It's a great book. I had the honour of being at the first McGill Summer School organised by Joe Mulholland of RTE. My mother actually knew Patrick McGill when he was a labouring man on the land in a place called Youngs of the Hollow. My mother was the daughter of a small farmer from a place near Drumquin. The first time I was banned by the Irish Censorship Board – I had the honour three times later on – I was so high and I was reading *The Rat Pit* by Patrick McGill. My mother took it from me saying, 'I don't think you're quite the age for reading *The Rat Pit* yet'. What was puzzling me about the story at the time was that at the end of one chapter the girl is listening to a fiddler playing *Swanee River* in an old bothy in Scotland and in the next chapter she is having a baby. I couldn't work out the connection between *Swanee River,* the fiddler and the baby. At that point the book was removed from me. I found out later on that there wasn't an exact connection: the girl had been going out with a young man at the time of listening to the fiddler. My brother-in-law Brian Coll, father of Brian Coll the singer, told a story about Youngs of the Hollow where McGill worked. Young of the Hollow would feed his labouring men on dry bread and one day one of the men said to him, 'Mr Young, did you never hear of jam, or butter or treacle?' So Young said, 'Do you say the Lord's Prayer boys?' 'We do', replied the labourmen. 'Well,' said Young, 'in the Lord's Prayer it says 'Give us this day our daily bread'. It doesn't say anything about jam or butter or treacle!'

Thomas Flanagan, the Irish-American academic and novelist, is a very good friend of yours. You have his latest novel 'The End of the Hunt' hot off the presses.

We are old friends. We were introduced by another American, now alas dead, Professor Kevin Sullivan, who's in a story of mine *The Dogs in the Great Glen*. The first time Tom Flanagan came over here he went out on the roads of Ireland with Sean J. White and myself but, boy, did he study the roads of Ireland on his own after that. That new book is absolutely weird because it brings the history of Ireland up to the 1920s. He knows every corner of Ireland and he brings the characters completely to life. It's absolutely incredible the amount of research he put into the book. The Civil War period is so vividly recreated you begin to feel you were there in the middle of it. Tom Flanagan didn't miss a corner or a boreen in his travels and research in Ireland.

Here's a well thumbed volume bespeaking traces of an earlier civilization. It's 'The Golden Ass' by Apuleius, the second century Roman author.

This goes back to the Old Roman Empire. It tells of the adventures and humiliation of the unfortunate man who was turned into a donkey. It's hilarious. Apuleius had written on witchcraft and various scholarly matters of his own time. The bookplate pasted into this copy of *The Golden Ass* reminds me that it was presented to me by a friend and it bears the coat of arms of Omagh town: you have the two rivers meeting in the middle of it and various symbols surrounding it.

Another prominent book on your shelves is 'The Works of Father Prout'.

He was, of course, Reverend Francis Sylvester Mahony, who is best know for that poem *The Bells of Shandon* that everybody sings but he wrote various literary treatises. He wrote a lot of verse and he satirises very effectively. I mean *The Rogueries of Tom Moore* is a wicked piece of work. He was rather rough too on Daniel O'Connell, the Liberator. He was a great classical scholar and a very strange man who haunted London in the company of Thackeray and boys like that. He travelled Europe a good deal and was an accomplished linguist.

Do you find now in your seventies that you are re-reading old favourites rather than tackling new works?

I always have to have a reason for going back. Maybe it's to check some quotation I've forgotten and that I need for some purpose or another. You go back to old books looking for some fact or figure or quotation. I don't just re-read sentimentally. Life is too short and it's getting shorter at 75!

You've been known throughout your life for your prodigious memory for ballads and songs. Was that a gift you always had?

It wasn't intelligence or anything like that. It was a gift for a circus like Mr Memory. I had a freak memory for things like that. I mean, if I read a poem twice, I could then recite it. It saved me a lot of trouble in class and a lot of hard work trying to learn the darn poems. Curiously enough, it remains and things I haven't read or thought of for years will come back to me again.

Who , of the younger generation Irish writers, do you read and admire?

Well to begin with, Seamus Heaney, John Montague and Thomas Kinsella. I wouldn't call them exactly young although they are younger than me. There is a great deal of good writing going on in Ireland at the moment both in prose and in poetry and at my age, it is a full-time job keeping up with new books published.

13

TIM PAT COOGAN

Tim Pat Coogan, historian and journalist, was born in Dublin and for twenty years was editor of *The Irish Press*. As a journalist he travelled extensively, covering the Vietnam War and interviewing such international figures as Colonel Gadaffi and Ronald Reagan. He has lectured widely at home and abroad on Irish affairs and has been a frequent international commentator on television and radio. His publications include *Ireland Since the Rising*, *The IRA*, *On the Blanket*, *The Irish: A Personal View* and acclaimed biographies of Michael Collins and Eamon De Valera.

Tim Pat Coogan, the first two volumes I see here on your shelves are Piaras Beaslaí's 'Michael Collins and the Making of a New Ireland'. Michael Collins is a figure who has had a profound impact on your life and on your work as a historian.

Indeed, and so had Piaras Beaslaí. I had heard a lot about Collins from older colleagues of my father, notably David Nelligan and others over the years. Mickey Rooney, the former Editor of *The Irish Independent*, told me about this extraordinary episode when he was called to the Governor's Wing in Crumlin Road Jail where he was imprisoned during the Civil War, to be told by the Governor that Collins had been shot. So he came back out onto the iron staircase and began to announce the news to his fellow prisoners. He was interrupted by the sound of the rosary as they all went down simultaneously on their knees, both Free Staters and Republicans in Crumlin Road Jail. The same story, or a variation of it is told by Tom Barry – Collins had that mesmeric effect. Those two volumes by Piaras Beaslaí I first came across when I was writing my first book, *Ireland Since the Rising*, back in 1965. I left *The Evening Press* after work at about four o'clock, went up to the National Library, got these two volumes out and settled in to read them. Some hours later I was touched on the shoulder by an attendant and was told they were closing as it was ten o'clock. I was completely absorbed in Beaslaí's volumes. I wanted to buy them but they were very difficult to get. Eventually, the late Tom Kenny of Galway's famous bookshop got them for me for ten pounds.

Beside them I see 'The Love Poems of William Butler Yeats'.

I've always been interested in Yeats. I remember at the launch of Ben Kiely's novel *Nothing Happens in Carmincross* I met Barbara Hayley, later Professor of English at Maynooth and she introduced me to the Yeats' scholar, A. Norman Jeffares.

He rekindled my interest in Yeats and I thought that the edition he did of *The Collected Poems of W. B. Yeats* for Macmillan was the best introduction anybody could have to Yeats. Not alone was the selection of poems wonderful, but he had marvellously illuminating notes at the back including everything from the pronunciation of words to the local topography, and from bits of history to who the characters were. I thought it was a model book. These lines of Yeats from *A Last Confession* are among my favourites.

> I gave what other women gave
> That stepped out of their clothes,
> But when this soul, its body off,
> Naked to naked goes
> He it has found shall find therein
> What none other knows.

You are also a big fan of the poetry of Seamus Heaney and I see you have his early volume 'Field Work' on your shelves.

Seamus Heaney is a wonderful man and a wonderful poet. He writes about things we can identify with. Apart from that he is blessed with his personality in that he is a very pleasant person. He is a very enabling man who gives his time very generously and he is also very lucky in that he has come to his maturity in a very benign time for the poet in Ireland. When you consider the reception his work and his personality have met in

Ireland compared to the reception given, and the expected behaviour of, writers like Patrick Kavanagh, Brendan Behan and Myles na Gopaleen then Seamus Heaney is blessed. They got no economic support but wrote for peanuts. There was terrific drinking and self-destruction. It's amazing Kavanagh lived as long as he did. The artist destroyed by Dublin is the leitmotif that runs through the lives of so many of these writers. Seamus Heaney escaped all that. He is a good model of Yeats's dictum: 'Irish poets, learn your trade'. He certainly did that. In this poem, *Casualty*, Heaney writes about Northern Ireland after the shootings in Derry on Bloody Sunday when the walls said 'Paras Thirteen – Bogside Nil'. There was great hatred of anybody who was seen to give aid or support to the troops. The man in this poem wouldn't give in to the threats to stay home, and here Heaney gives us insights into both sides of the terror. He talks about this man who defied his own people to go out.

> But he would not be held
> At home by his own crowd
> Whatever threats were phoned,
> Whatever black flags waved.
> I see him as he turned
> In that bombed offending place,
> Remorse fused with terror
> In his still knowable face,
> His cornered outfaced stare
> Blinding in the flesh.

As a former newspaper editor and longtime journalist I know you have great admiration for Alistair Cooke and I see his volume 'The Americans: Letters from America 1969 – 79' on your shelves.

Alistair Cooke is an extraordinary character. I suspect he grew up as something of a snob. He was always at the very best tables and married an Admiral's daughter. He had an entrée to society from a very high level. Instead of just degenerating into gossip, however, he became probably the most penetrating critic and affectionate reporter on America of his day. His other book, *Alistair Cooke's America*, is full of insights, ranging from little anecdotes about people he knows living in the Twinkle Toes Sandy Motel to meetings with President Kennedy. He has, of course, what is essential for any journalist – energy, accuracy, great professionalism and a sense of humour. I would certainly commend him to the younger school of journalists. His *Sunday Morning Letter from America* on BBC Radio is wonderful.

He works in a circular, circuitous way. His radio essay might begin, 'I want to tell you today about a man but first let me say', and he goes on for fourteen minutes and in the last thirty seconds he sums everything up and says, 'and that was the man who was shot before my very eyes'. He is the transatlantic equivalent of Ben Kiely who goes in a circumlocutary way all around the Lagan Valley, and then finally comes back to closing time in Mulligan's where the anecdote began. Cooke also builds up to a punchline, and has a wonderful radio voice.

In your 'Irish Press' days you knew Brendan Behan well and you have here his 'Complete Plays' introduced by Alan Simpson. It is so difficult now to separate Behan, the man from the myth.

It is, indeed, very hard to separate them. He would certainly be one of the artist destroyed figures. He felt the headlong rush was the only thing. He had to psych himself up very often for appearances, and the way to do that, he felt, was to be drunk. He interrupted plays in the West End shouting from the audience and this brought headlines in the *Daily Mail,* and that brought box-office success.

I knew him very well and more often sober than drunk because we were both very fond of swimming. He would often come out and I'd meet him down at the Forty Foot in Sandycove or on Killiney Beach. Beatrice, his wife, would walk behind him carrying the knapsack, probably containing bottles of Guinness and the sandwiches and the flask. She'd be carrying that and he'd be walking out in front of her waving his arms, heading to the nearest pub. That interlude of Alan Simpson and the Pike Theatre in Dublin was very important in my formative years. I saw the opening night of *The Quare Fellow* there. Behan was there, as usual, pretty well on with a good two days' of stubble, no tie, a good suit but you wouldn't know whether he was trying to get into it or get out of it, and the shirt just about hanging on him. We knew the play was a hit and there were loud cries of 'Author, author!' He came out on stage and said, 'I want to sing a song from my favourite dramatist' and he sang *Red Roses for Me* by Sean O'Casey. Then he went off. That was the sort of anti-climactic thing he did. He was very fortunate that he met Joan Littlewood. He said to me himself that he had written *An Giall* but she turned it into a hit play called *The Hostage* and he was under no illusion about her contribution to his success.

Alan Simpson said rather caustically once that the nice thing about watching Niall Toibin playing Behan in 'Borstal Boy' was that you could watch him and enjoy him but it was a relief not to have to go back and meet Brendan afterwards.

That is certainly the case and the bottle destroyed him. The stories are funny now, such as the story told where, once overcome by emotion and patriotism at a funeral in Glasnevin, he grabbed a revolver from either a Special Branch man or one of the IRA firing party and opened fire on the Special Branch. He got 14 years for this and Behan's father, who was telling me this anecdote said, 'Yeah, one year for every effin' foot he missed him by!'

14

JOHN O'CONOR

John O'Conor, concert pianist, was educated at University College Dublin and the Hochschule Für Musik in Vienna. He is Professor of Piano at the Royal Academy of Music and was Co-Founder and Artistic Director of the GPA Dublin International Piano Competition. As a concert pianist he has played with such world famous orchestras as the Vienna Symphony, Czech Philharmonic, Royal Philharmonic, NHK Orchestra of Tokyo and the Symphonies of Cleaveland, Detroit, Montreal and Washington DC. He has made many acclaimed recordings including John Field's Concertos, Sonatas and Nocturnes, Beethoven's Piano Sonatas, Mozart's Piano Concertos as well as works by Chopin and Schumann. By his frequent tours abroad he has become an Irish ambassador of music.

John O'Conor, poetry was your first love. How did that come about?

When I was a kid, my mother sent us to everything to see if we would be good at anything. I was sent to learn piano and my sisters to do ballet. One of the things she did was to send us to a speech and drama class at the Burke School of Elocution which used to be in Kildare Street. Miss Burke was a wonderful teacher who taught poetry and drama and all sorts of things. I was in the same class as Joe Dowling and the late lamented Tony Hennigan who was killed about ten years ago. It was fascinating the way Miss Burke would talk about poetry, and what was going on behind it. It wasn't enough just to learn the words. I remember seeing Brenda Fricker come in – she was preparing for some examination or other. She was doing James Stephens' poem *The Snare* and the rest of the class had to sit down and listen. It was just riveting. The power of the words became fascinating to me and attracted me very much. Then I remember doing my first Yeats poem, *The Stolen Child*.

Come away, human child!
To the waters and the wild
With a fairy, hand in hand,
For the world's more full of weeping
than you can understand.

I was only eleven at the time, and I'm sure I didn't understand it all that much. At the same time, the mystery of it and the imagery and the colourful way Yeats described Sligo were always fascinating to me.

Of contemporary Irish poets I see you have the works of Seamus Heaney on your shelves, in particular 'Station Island'.

I think I have bought more copies of *Station Island* than anybody because in travelling around I meet an awful lot of people who talk about Ireland and poetry and I say to them, 'Have you read *Station Island?*' and I come home and send them a copy. He is a great poet. He has a wonderful use of language and the range of emotion he can talk about, from the death of his brother to the troubles in the North to the land fascination, is astonishing.

You are a great reader of contemporary Irish fiction. Among the many Irish volumes I see here is John McGahern's 'Amongst Women'.

I love to buy Irish writers and I try to buy them in hardback in the hope that by supporting them in this way they will keep on writing. I think *Amongst Women* is one of the most amazing stories and yet, in some ways, a very simple story. It's a very typical story about Ireland and I think the way McGahern writes about Ireland is what attracts me most to him. I also love Bernard McLaverty's novel *Lamb* because it was my son Hugh's first major movie. I'd actually read some McLaverty before that and loved him. James Plunkett's *Strumpet City* is another great Irish novel of the century. I've known Jim for years – he's a wonderful violinist. He interviewed me for *The Irish Times* soon after I came back from Vienna and we became friendly. I think *Strumpet City* is a great novel. I have a lot of books about Dublin including Anthony Cronin's *Dead As Doornails* which is a fascinating story about the time when Dublin seems to have been at its most raunchy and bawdy. Literary Dublin in the 1940s and '50s seems to have been extraordinary and Cronin gives a wonderful description of it. I would like to have lived in Dublin at that time except I would probably always have been broke. There was no money for music then and the chances of making a living were minute. The writers didn't seem to need money and always seem to have had enough for a few pints.

I see you have all the novels of Maeve Binchy including her collection of early journalism 'My First Book'.

I think that, like most people, I was first attracted to Maeve Binchy by her journalism. She became a household name for readers of *The Irish Times*. When you thought about going out to a dinner party or sitting on a bus you realised the way Maeve would record those overheard conversations made them sound fascinating. People would start quoting her and likening experiences by saying, 'God, it's as if Maeve Binchy had written it'. I had read most of the articles from *My First Book* when they appeared in the newspaper but I had missed one. It was about going skiing and I remember the first sentence: 'I expected to fall when I went skiing but I didn't expect to fall as I came out of the railway station'. The tears were pouring down my face with laughter. I remember I met Maeve some years ago and I told her I still had *My First Book*. 'Did you buy that?' she asked, 'I think I have three thousand copies of it under my bed at home.' It's a wonderful book and a marvellous read and should be reprinted.

You are a regular theatre-goer, I know, and I see you have a copy of Brian Friel's play 'Dancing at Lughnasa', a play that struck a chord with so many people around the world. Why do you think it was so successful from Glenties to Broadway?

I'm not sure. Of course, it's a wonderful play and Brian Friel is a masterful playwright. Maybe the extra dimension of the Irish dancing and the fascination of the radio struck a chord because people can recognise that around the world. The play is about rural life in Ireland in the 1930s yet it has universal appeal and recognition. I don't know why a play like *Translations* hasn't travelled just as well: I think it's an extraordinary play and I'd love to see it performed more.

I'm slightly surprised to see you are a fan of Dick Francis – I wouldn't have thought you were into the horsey world.

I'm not horsey in the slightest. I just think he's a fantastic read. I've got all his books. Maybe it's an indication of their huge literary merit that I can't always remember the story-lines which is wonderful because you can go back and read them all over again. I've always enjoyed what people would call 'less-than-high' literature. I don't see why one should be highbrow about reading only literature all the time.

Charles Dickens was one of the great mass-appeal popular writers of his day and 'Oliver Twist' is one of your favourite novels.

I love Charles Dickens. I started trying to read *David Copperfield* when I was about ten and just couldn't because I thought it was too difficult. I saw the film of *A Tale of Two Cities*, became hooked on Dickens, and went on to read a lot of the other novels. It was the same with the Russians, including Dostoyevsky. Once you get past the first hundred pages and remember who the characters are and can distinguish between them, it's plain sailing.

Another great storyteller in the Irish tradition was Walter Macken and I see you have 'Seek the Fair Land', his novel about Ireland in Cromwellian times.

He was a great story-teller and that novel is part of a marvellous trilogy. Macken tells the history of Ireland in novel form from Cromwell right up to the Civil War this century. He stimulated my interest in Irish history. I'm fascinated by the way the two cultures in Ireland drifted apart and I've read a lot about Irish Catholicism and Protestantism in the last century.

In your career as a musician do you read a lot of the biographies and backgrounds of the composers you perform?

Yes, I do read an enormous amount and you have to, I think, to understand the music. Nowadays, I find reading about performance practices and interpretation more interesting than new biographies of composers which, by and large, regurgitate the same facts. The more I know about Chopin or John Field and the world about them – what they were reading, what art they were seeing and what was happening historically – the more I understand their music. When you play the Chopin ballads you have to understand the terrible situation Poland was in at the time and what gave him inspiration. As a performer I always like to know as much as I can about the whole social and cultural background of the composer I am playing.

15

NUALA NÍ DHOMHNAILL

Nuala Ní Dhomhnaill was born in England to Irish parents but grew up in the Gaeltacht of West Kerry and Tipperary. She was educated at University College Cork and spent seven years living abroad in Turkey and Holland. Her poetry, written in Irish, is filled with incisive descriptions of nature, with explorations of the reality of the lives of women in contemporary Ireland, and with images drawn from mythology, folklore and the female psyche, which she calls Hag Energy. She has published three collections of poetry in Irish, *An Dealg Droighín* (1981), *Féar Suaithinseach* (1984) and *Feis* (1994). Her *Selected Poems* (1986) were translated by Michael Hartnett, and The Gallery Press has published two bilingual selections, *Pharaoh's Daughter* (1990) and *The Astrakhan Cloak* (1992).

Nuala Ní Dhomhnaill, the first book I see on your shelves is James Joyce's 'A Portrait of the Artist as a Young Man', which, I believe, was an eye-opener for you when you first read it.

I was very young when I read it, only about fourteen and I remember I was given out to for reading it at the time because girls of fourteen weren't supposed to read that sort of thing. It was one of those books that had a huge effect on me. I think what that book did more than anything else was that it brought whole parts of my own life, which had been lived in a sort of para-literary sphere, into a different area altogether where suddenly there was the stuff of which literature is made. Little things like where Stephen Dedalus is in Clongowes Wood College and he writes on his copybook:

Stephen Dedalus
Class of Elements, Clongowes Wood College
Sallins, County Kildare
Ireland
Europe
The Universe

We used to do that and I see my own kids doing it from about the age of eight to ten. To see this in a book made me feel that my life was the sort of stuff of which literature was made. That was a marvellous eye-opener. Of course it is very much the Irish young person's *Bildungsroman*. There were other wonderful things too – like when Stephen goes down to Cork with his father Mr Dedalus sings:

> For love is teasin' and love is pleasin'
> And love is pleasure when first it's new
> But as love grows older then love grows colder
> And fades away with the morning dew.

My father used to sing that around the house and again it made me aware that literature wasn't something out there belonging to other people. It was mine as well. Except, of course, *Portrait of the Artist as a Young Man* was the wrong book to be living in. When we were young, female experience was totally subsumed into male experience. This was the *Bildungsroman* of our generation but the artist was a young man. It took me years to find its female equivalent, and I should have found it earlier but of course it was banned. It was set in the same school where I was a boarder in Limerick, only sixty years later. This was Kate O'Brien's novel *The Land of Spices*. It's a young woman's *Bildungsroman* which is so very different to the *Portrait* in that what a young man has to do, according to Joyce, is to break free from the nets of Mother Ireland and go forth to create his own soul. What Kate O'Brien seems to be saying is the opposite: what young women have to do is to make connections, create the webs. For a good fifteen or twenty years of my life I was living in the wrong book. Kate O'Brien's name was unmentionable when I was at boarding school in Laurel Hill Convent in Limerick. The regime at boarding school which she describes and the one we experienced sixty years later were almost identical. The only differences were that they used to have their prize-givings on Friday evenings and we used have ours on Sunday mornings, and they spoke French between gongs whereas we spoke English. Apart from that it was the exact same regime sixty years down the road. Years later, having been in Turkey, I came across *The Land of Spices* and read it in a Bed and Breakfast in Galway and couldn't leave it down until two or three o'clock in the morning. Actually, it made me very depressed, because it brought home the huge difference between the life I had been leading at seventeen and the life I was leading at twenty-seven. The next day, hitching back to Kerry, I wrote a poem called *Leaba Shióda*, which I suppose was my way of coming to terms with *The Land of Spices*.

I see you have the poetry of John Berryman on your shelves, and you told me his poetry saved your life at one time.

It would not be an exaggeration to say that. I had the first and maybe one of the worst of my cyclic depressions when I was nineteen. It was a reactive depression and I lost four stone in weight in four months. I nearly didn't recover. Everything became totally meaningless; books especially, as Hamlet would say, became just 'words, words, words'. One day Greg O'Donoghue handed me John Berryman's *77 Dream Songs* and I opened it and read: 'I am outside, incredible panic rules.' Suddenly I realised: my God, somebody else has been where I am. One of the great poems in that collection about the art of writing, which I found wonderfully meaningful at the time, contains the lines:

> I am obliged to perform in complete darkness
> Operations of great delicacy on myself.

It's the sense of terror and threat that meant an awful lot to me in the state I was in at that time. I felt I had fallen out of the known world, gone off the edge of the world where mariners used to talk about the sun falling off the edge in medieval times. They could hear this awful roar at the edge of the world. John Berryman hauled me back from that edge. Shapespeare's sonnets and John Berryman are somehow juxtaposed in my life: when I start thinking about one I reread the other. When I'm writing poems myself I find that when you find a Berryman echo in a poem you are sure to find a Shakespeare echo in the same poem. I do use books as life savers. I use books as a way of creating an epistemological net for myself so that I can launch myself into the great unknown. That's what every poem is, a sheep's leap in the deep. It helps to have some sort of theoretical framework to underpin you.

At what stage did you discover the literature of the Blasket Islands – Peig Sayers, Muiris Ó Súilleabháin, Tomás Ó Criomtháin?

I didn't have to discover them: they were given. These were books that were in the house when I was growing up. My mother is from West Kerry and she is a sister of An tAthair Pádraig Ó Fiannachta, and he had a large influence on our lives as we were growing up. There were always books about the Blaskets around because half of our relations were out there. They still come back to be buried in Ventry: a lot of the graves in St Catherine's graveyard, where I hope to be buried myself, are island graves. Greater scholars than I have tried to explain the fine flowering of literature in the Blaskets at the beginning of this century. I would think it was a mixture of different things. The character of Tomás Ó Criomthain, who wrote *The Islandman,* had a lot to do with it. He actually taught himself to read Irish on the mainland from these proselytising books that the Irish Missionary Society brought out. Then, the ball started rolling and all these scholars coming in from the outside, like Robin Flower, gave the islanders a way of feeling detached about themselves which maybe people on the mainland didn't have. In a way, the Irish on the mainland was as authentic: it's just that there wasn't this mythicisation of the mainland. I dragged all these Blasket authors off to Turkey with me, read them, and after seven years dragged them all the way back again.

You are a great reader of international contemporary fiction, and I see you have the Japanese Nobel Prize-winner, Kenzaburo Oe's novel 'Silent Cry' on your shelves.

I was in Japan this year and I like the Japanese writer Shusako Endo. My Japanese translator said to me that I'd love Oe, long before the Nobel Prize was announced. The reason I like writers like Oe is that basically I am a misanthrope. I'm not racist or sectarian or sexist: I just hate the human race across the board. Fortunately, or unfortunately, I get very fond of individuals, but on the whole I think we're just a cancer on the face of the globe. I rarely find that very deep feeling expressed anywhere, so when I come across it in another writer I think, 'Oh wonderful, somebody is telling the truth at last!' This other book, Thomas Bernhardt's *Woodcutters*, translated from the German, gives a wonderful insight into the human soul and into all the negative side of life which, I think, is glossed over too easily. I'm looking for books that tell me the way I look at the world isn't totally bananas. In the dominant discourse I don't find that, but I do find that modern fiction is a great help.

You're also a voracious reader of philosophy, psychology, theology and feminist theory. I see a volume here called 'God Is a Trauma: Vicarious Religion and Soul Making' by Greg Morgenson.

This book basically expresses the fact that in many ways what you don't understand you deify. If something hits you that is too big for you, like child sexual abuse, this becomes the thing that people make into a god. Therefore, God becomes a punitive, frightening thing. I have a lot of books which hope to deal with that rather difficult subject. These would all be in the Jungian archetypal psychology line. I don't subscribe to any particular psychological school but these are useful scaffolding on which I can write another poem. I'm not going to turn out books on theology or philosophy. When I read all this stuff I start muttering to myself as a result. When I start muttering to myself in Irish it comes out as poems; when I start muttering to myself in English it comes out as polemic. I've decided now I've a good line in polemic: basically what you are missing by not having Irish. Anything that feeds that is grist to the mill.

16

TERRY KEANE

Terry Keane, one of Ireland's most widely read and controversial columnists, was born in England and educated at Trinity College Dublin. She has worked as a journalist and fashion editor for *The Irish Times*, *The Sunday Press* and currently is fashion editor and social diarist for the *Sunday Independent*. She has made her column 'The Keane Edge' a source of amusement and apoplexy in households across the country on Sunday mornings. Her first book, *Consuming Passions*, a mixture of recipes and accounts of high social living, was published in 1994 by Blackwater Press. She lists as her hobbies 'living, loving and the corridors of power'.

Terry Keane, the first book I see here on your shelves is an enormously fat novel of the twentieth century, and it has an intriguing, if somewhat shocking, opening sentence.

It is Anthony Burgess's *Earthly Powers,* and I think it has the most riveting opening sentence of any novel: 'It was the afternoon of my eighty-first birthday, and I was in bed with my catamite when Ali announced that the archbishop had come to see me.' Now, I mean, beat that! But it is a wonderful novel. It's a large, sprawling novel about two very powerful men, one in the literary world and one in the Church who ends up being Pope. It takes you all over the world on a literary voyage. You have Æ, George Russell, making love in Buswell's Hotel in Dublin, and then you switch to Monaco and London. It is a marvellously rich book. I shall miss Anthony Burgess and I miss the fact and lament that we won't have any more from him. His prose style was so riveting. I loved the security of starting a big novel like *Earthly Powers* and knowing you were going to be entranced for days.

I know you like political diaries, and the juicier and more gossipy they are the better. I see you have English politician Alan Clark's Diaries here.

Yes, they were splendid. They are so indiscreet. I have a passion for diaries. I think they are one of the most wonderful forms of literature. I think Alan Clark is so rude, so impossible and exasperating, and so lovable at the same time. I remember phoning him about something and being rather disapproving of him and his attitude towards women, but by the time I had finished the phone call I was totally in love and enchanted by him. He is like a little schoolboy cocking a snook at all the other cabinet ministers. He brings them down to size. I'm sure he is unfair about a lot of them but it does make a very good read.

Are you disappointed that more Irish politicians haven't published their diaries?

I'm very glad that some of them haven't, actually!

You have Andrew Sinclair's biography of the Irish-born painter, Francis Bacon.

Francis Bacon was a marvellous man. I was very lucky to have had the opportunity of meeting him in London with Garech Browne and spending a complete day and almost a night with him. We had a typical day in the life of Francis Bacon, starting in the French House pub and then going on to the Colony Club. He was the most incredible-looking man I think I've ever seen. He had the most mesmerising face and was very beautiful. I like Sinclair's biography because it was written by someone who had done a lot of research and liked the man very much. It is a very balanced book. In the time I spent with Bacon I saw him in all his moods, from truculence to philosophising to talking about Ireland and the people he knew, and his memoirs. It was just like opening a curtain and seeing this rich life, because he was an artist with words too. He was a wonderful raconteur.

I see you have Dominick Dunne's novel 'People Like Us'. Do you like this novel because it chronicles the lives of a particular social set?

I'm quite fascinated by New York society. I think Dominick Dunne is an excellent writer, and he loathes being compared with Truman Capote but I think he is very like Capote. He is irreverent, he is honest, he is furious and angry. But he moves in that society, so he is not like someone looking in from the outside: he is part of that glittering set. He despises their morals and the way they get away with murder, literally, in some of his novels.

Beside that witty novel with a whiff of scandal I see a serious book about art and artists. It is Robert Hughes's 'Nothing If Not Critical'.

I like him because he is an iconoclast who blasts everyone and everything. I think more than anything he is the kind of critic who teaches you how to look at a painting. He teaches, but not in a ponderous way. He is very perceptive and very, very witty. So even though this is a serious book it pulls down accepted images, questions reputations and sometimes takes a very opposite view from the establishment's view, which I suppose reflects my style as well.

Since you are a connoisseur of the good life, I'm not surprised to see Peter Mayle's 'Expensive Habits' on your shelves. Is that your guide to gracious living?

It proves that the best things in life are not free. He talks about second homes and mistresses and private jets and caviar and cashmere. He has a marvellous chapter on Paris and it's as if he was following me. We have exactly the same taste. He's lucky enough to have written a bestseller so he can afford it. I intend to do the same one of these days. I would love to meet Peter Mayle, and I'm surprised I haven't bumped into him in one of the top spots in the world. His views on Havana cigars and hundred-dollar haircuts and handmade shoes completely coincide with my views on the good life.

Moving across the room to your Irish library, I see classics from the Blasket Islands.

There are three great classics from the Blasket Islands – there's the autobiography of Peig Sayers, Maurice O'Sullivan's *Twenty Years A-Growing* and Tomás Ó Criomtháin's *The Islandman*. I think *The Islandman* is my favourite because it is very simply written. The tone of the book is almost as if he is taking you into a corner and whispering in your ear. He is reflecting very simply and very honestly. At the end of the book he says:

> I have written minutely of much that we did for it is my wish that somewhere there should be a memorial of it all and I have done my best to set down the character of the people about me so that some record of us might live after us. For the like of us will never be again.

I think that last sentence has often been misinterpreted. What he is saying is that he is writing about the disappearance of a society. He is not boasting that we are so unbelievable that there will never again be people like us. It's a lament for a disappearing era. I think this mood is reflected too in his statue in Dunquin in Kerry where he has the book in his hand and he is turned towards the Blasket Islands. He is actually shunning the future and looking longingly at the past. It is the simplicity and integrity of these people that we have lost today, and I think we are harking back in some sort of spiritual sense to those bygone values. I think everybody should read *The Islandman* often.

I see Brendan Kennelly's volume 'Love of Ireland: Poems from the Irish' beside it.

I love everything Brendan writes and I have all his books. I think this simple book represents Brendan at his best, and his translation of 'The Old Woman of Beare' is beautiful.

The sea crawls from the shore
Leaving there
The despicable weed,
A corpse's hair.
In me,
The desolate withdrawing sea.

The Old Woman of Beare am I
Who once was beautiful.
Now all I know is how to die
I'll do it well.

I also like Richard Murphy's poetry very much. Wasn't it Yeats who wrote that one day he would like to write a poem 'as cold and passionate as the dawn'. I think Richard Murphy does write like that. He has this very controlled sonnet form, very rigid, yet the depth of his passion does come through. He writes about all these monuments that signify important times in his life. I love his poem 'Red Bank Restaurant' where he went to dinner with Conor Cruise O'Brien and Richard Murphy's wife.

His cruiser eyes, when not nailed to her cross
By mother wit, fled exiled through the bar:
Soon to be reconciled, screened by clear glass,
As he smiled at his cold brilliance mirrored there.

That's devastating! *The Price of Stone* by Richard Murphy would be my desert island book.

17

JOHN B. KEANE

John B. Keane, playwright, novelist, short-story writer and essayist, was born in Listowel, County Kerry, where he still lives. His plays are epitomised by strong plots and characters depicting life in rural Ireland combined with salty, witty dialogue. His greatest successes have been *Sive*, *The Field* (made into a film in 1991), *Big Maggie*, *The Year of the Hiker*, *Sharon's Grave*, *Many Young Men of Twenty* and *Moll*. He has published a successful novel, *The Bodhrán Makers*, and several comic collections in his *Letters* series. He was conferred with a Doctorate of Literature by Trinity College, Dublin, is a past President of Irish PEN and a member of Aosdana. He is a frequent broadcaster and an engaging and witty raconteur.

We're sitting in a room over the most famous pub in Listowel – in fact one of the most famous in Ireland. It's a book-lined room, the study of one of Ireland's most acclaimed and popular writers. John B. Keane, when you were growing up in Listowel, was it a town which respected books and the written word?

It really did. There was no scarcity of books. There may have been, in my boyhood, a scarcity of money and, often for the poor, a scarcity of food and downright poverty. I remember when I was going to school seeing the signs of malnutrition on my schoolmates quite clearly because you could see the scabs on their heads which were shaved to the bone. This was all due to improper diet. But there was no scarcity of books in the school that time, because the County Library came once a week and you could select your books. I remember probably the first book I ever read was called *In Texas with Davy Crockett and Sam Houston*. I must have read that seven or eight times altogether. I wouldn't have been any more than nine or ten that time. Then I graduated and my next book was my first love as a novel, and it was to remain my true love until very nearly the end of my days now. That book was *Treasure Island* by Robert Louis Stevenson. I think that *Treasure Island* can be read five times with positive returns in a person's lifetime. You can read it first of all when you are a child. You can read it when you are a young. You can read it when you are middle-aged. Finally, you can read it most profitably of all when you are an old dodderer, because *Treasure Island* is a book for all ages. It's one of the great adventure stories. It is very whimsical and full of the most colourful characters I've ever encountered in any novel in my lifetime. Take Long John Silver alone, who is the greatest rogue and the most lovable rascal in literature. He has no peer. Who, I ask you, is more colourful that Ben Gunn when he suddenly confronts Jim Hawkins and asks him that memorable question: 'Have you a bit of cheese?' So you can see we had a great advantage in the town of Listowel with teachers like Bryan McMahon. My own father had a fine library at home in his house and, even when money was scarce, books were not. I had all Dickens read, I'd say, by the time I was sixteen. I read Scott and knew *Ivanhoe* inside out. But *Treasure Island* was my favourite because it's a marvellous book. It's so well written and there isn't a single cardboard character in it. Every one of them is solid – the backbone of the English countryside and the scum of the sea.

There's a very different author on your shelves – Zane Grey.

Zane Grey's *Riders of the Purple Sage* is a great romantic yarn, a great love story, a story about fast horses and slow horses. Zane Grey was the beloved of every boy in my time. Then of course there was *The Cisco Kid*, and I'll always remember a chapter from one of his adventures when the Cisco Kid is asked by a very dangerous bandit to fight with his fists. The Cisco Kid says to him, 'Señor, if I fight I hurt my hands. If I hurt my hand I cannot play the guitar, and if I cannot play the guitar, Señor, I cannot make love to the señorita.'

Your love of adventure stories has prevailed. Over there I see 'The Cruel Sea' by Nicholas Monsarrat.

The Cruel Sea is the great sea novel of the war, along with *The Caine Mutiny* by Herman Wouk. Somebody once argued that *The Cruel Sea* was an officer's book. Well, it was written by an officer but it isn't an officer's book. It was the best book to come out of the war. It's a great story about sea captains and courage at sea. There is one chapter that begins: 'Some men died bravely and some men died like cowards.' Some died in total sorrow and others died futilely, thinking of lost loves. Other fellows who had made a mess of their lives couldn't care less. The real tragedy was in the youth who were drowned who had so much to give. It's a great dramatic account of drowning after your ship has gone down. I suspect that Herman Wouk's *The Caine Mutiny* was strongly influenced by Monsarrat, because I believe there is no truly original song or book or anything. There was a great trial at the end of *The Caine Mutiny*, and what I loved about that book was that there was a character in it to challenge any dramatist's creation. As a playwright and as an aspiring playwright I saw the character of Keefer, the embryonic novelist who wrote multitudes. He was a shifty character. He was brilliant, he was gregarious, he was fun-loving, but he was shifty and you couldn't trust him. The other men aboard the ship were friends who were prepared to die for each other but Keefer was always watching out for Keefer. It never emerged until the very end of the book and this was a masterly piece of disguise by the novelist in question. It's a great book.

There's a book I don't know. It is by Halldor Laxness and is called 'Independent People'.

Wait till I take a swallow of this. You can't beat a couple of swallows of beer to clear the throat. It subdues the frogs in the windpipe. *Independent People* was the story of an Icelandic small farmer who was a hard case. He subjugated his wife and his son and his daughter to such a degree that they loathed him. He was a man who believed in the land, who believed that the totality of human existence was enshrined in land. He had great love for one particular gentleman in the book and he was Reverend Goodmonger, who had great rams and these rams then sired the hero's sheep and the ewes often had twins and triplets. Wherever he went he spoke with great love and affection of Goodmonger. Then he went away on a monumental journey of nearly three hundred miles to Reykjavik to buy a pedigree ram. When he went, his wife, who had been kept down all her life, killed a lamb. Together with her daughter and son she ate every bit of it. For them it was a great feast. When he came back he missed the lamb and he never spoke to his wife again. When she died he didn't put a stone over her but when his favourite ram died he put a beautiful headstone over him. This was a man who was too much of a realist, a man who put his sheep and his land before his womenfolk. It was a marvellous book because it showed us the hardship endured by Icelandic farmers down through the ages. There were great similarities between them and the Irish farmers. In fact they had it harder than the Irish small farmers who survived from the days of the Land League onwards. I was fascinated by that book. I remember the year that book came out, 1953, the Nobel Prize was won by Winston Churchill for his massive collection *The History of the English-Speaking Peoples*, which he didn't write, of course, but which he organised. It was the wrong decision. Several of us young fellows in the town at that time, led by John Joe Daly, now dead unfortunately, wrote letters to the papers about this. We were amazed to discover that all over the world there were other young men writing letters to the papers. The result was that the following year Halldor Laxness won the Nobel Prize for Literature, so we in Listowel had tremendous influence after all!

Your fellow townsman Byan McMahon features prominently on your shelves.

There's another great romantic writer. *The Honey Spike* is a masterpiece of its kind, the most delightful book. I bought it in Danny Flahivan's bookshop years ago where Bryan and Maurice Walsh and Seamus Wilmot and myself and several other eminent authors used to browse. There was one thing about Danny – if you didn't have the price of a book he would say, 'Take it away, boy. Bring it back when you've it read.' When Joyce's *Ulysses* was banned it was placed in a position of outstanding prominence in that bookshop window. In fact, the window was full of copies of *Ulysses*, while the book was banned. There was no censorship in Flahivan's. We were all astonished in Church Street, which was the street where I was born and where the bookshop was situated, when Walter Macken's *Quench the Moon* was banned. We couldn't comprehend it. Censorship is the most vile restriction that can be imposed on creative people, and I have stood against it all my life.

❧

18

DAVID MARCUS

David Marcus was born in Cork city and is a graduate of University College, Cork and King's Inns, Dublin. He practised at the Irish Bar for some years before founding and editing the prestigious quarterly *Irish Writing*. After thirteen years in London he returned to Dublin, where he started the New Irish Writing page in the *Irish Press* which became a national institution. As Literary Editor of the *Irish Press* he had an enormous influence on the development of young and emerging Irish writers. He has edited several anthologies of short stories, including *The Bodley Head Book of Irish Short Stories*. His first novel, *Next Year in Jerusalem*, was published in 1954, and since then he has published *A Land Not Theirs* and *A Land in Flames*. He has also published short stories and poetry, including a translation of Brian Merriman's epic poem *The Midnight Court*.

David Marcus, author, translator, literary editor and man of letters, you began collecting books at a very early age in your native Cork city.

Yes I did – from my early teens I think I was collecting books. Of course, at that time it was second-hand books and the early sixpenny Penguins. The second-hand books my two bothers and I used to buy in Joe Kerrigan's of Washington Street, and a lot of natives of Cork will remember that place with great fondness. The three of us collected books and we had a little problem, actually, because at home in Cork the bookcase was a very large open bookcase in the livingroom and it was full of our books. The problem was that friends of my father used come in, go up to the bookcase and see what caught their fancy. My father could never refuse his friends anything, so a book would go out of the house and, as a rule, would never come back. So my brothers and I were tearing our hair out over it and we got together and concocted a couplet which we wrote out in beautiful copperplate writing on a white card and pinned it up on the bookcase and the couplet said:

> The liberties of friendship don't extend
> To wives or books. These borrow not, nor lend.

It hadn't the slightest effect. Friends of my father used still walk up to the bookcase, look at the couplet, then chuckle and giggle and say, 'Very funny, very droll. Oh, may I have that?'

The books still kept disappearing, so we sat down, had another council of war and some one of us came up with the inspiration. We added just one word to the bottom of the couplet and we never had any more trouble. The word we added was 'Shakespeare'. They were afraid to go against the god.

I see you have a lot of books about your native Cork on your bookshelves. One that catches my eye is a book of pictures of Cork entitled 'Cork: City by the Lee'.

It's mainly in pictures I see Cork, because I rarely go back there, having left in 1954. The Cork I go back to now is not the Cork of my memory. The Cork of my memory, when it was so vital, so compact, means a great deal to me. I only have to look at these pictures and so many memories flood back to me. Here's a picture of the beautiful quadrangle in University College, Cork which I attended. When I went to UCC the famous Alfie O'Raghilly was boss there and Alfie, of course, was quite a genius. I was doing Law and I wanted to do Arts as well, so I signed up for both degrees. I was called to Alfie's study and he said to me, 'I see you are down for Law and Arts. Of course, there's nothing against you doing both together. But I'll tell you something – you won't get the exams!' I knew by the look in his eye what he was getting at, so I didn't do Law and Arts together.

This book by Colm Lincoln is also mostly pictures, and it's called *Steps and Steeples: Cork at the Turn of the Century*. In a way I prefer this book of pictures of Cork because they are all black and white, and somehow that is the way I like to remember Cork. There is one terribly interesting and wry picture in it showing that wonderful Pope's Quay and Saint Mary's Church, a huge church with a big ionic portico and six huge massive pillars holding up the roof. I remember one beautiful summer's day when I was about nine I was walking past that church and the Corpus Christi procession came along. The streets were thronged with people and the bishop and the priests in their vestments came along holding up the big Host in front of them. Just as they came abreast of me the people fell to their knees and of course, being Jewish, I wasn't familiar with that. I was terror-stricken because I was the only one left standing up. I didn't know what to do. I couldn't besmirch my own flag, being Jewish, so I just ran and hid behind one of those huge pillars. I suppose it's the only time a nine-year-old Jew took refuge in the Catholic Church.

You have a little volume here called 'The Jews in Ireland' by Bernard Shillmann.

Bernard Shillmann was my uncle, actually married to one of my mother's sisters, and he was a barrister specialising in workmen's compensation law in Ireland. He was a tremendous scholar both of Shakespeare and of Jewish history, and he wrote this brief but very valuable book on the Jews in Ireland. It was privately published by him and there are very few copies available. This book is a revelation. For instance, it was in this book that I learned that the wife of the famous Irish leader, William Smith O'Brien, was Jewish and she converted to the Catholic Church. Also in this book I learned that Charles Stewart Parnell's mother was Jewish. I found one little sentence which embedded itself in my memory and that sentence was: 'Around the turn of the century a small band of Jews in Cork planned to emigrate to Palestine but their plans fell through.' That sentence became the seed many years later that inspired me to write my novel *A Land Not Theirs*.

The great formative influence of your younger days was the Penguin paperback, of which you have hundreds on your shelves. One that has a special place in your affections is 'The Daring Young Man on the Flying Trapeze' by William Saroyan.

That collection of stories by Saroyan was the first collection that became lodged in my memory, and I think it's that collection that started off my passion for the short story. I read it in the Cork Public Library as a teenager. It was first published in 1935. It was so fresh, so different, so vital, so cheeky that it really showed me, even at that early age, what one could do with the short story. I followed Saroyan's writings ever afterwards. When I started the quarterly magazine called *Irish Writing* which I edited from 1945 onwards, I wrote to Saroyan and asked him if he would send me a story. Not only did he send one but he wrote one especially and he called it 'Four Hours for Irish Writing'. Many years later, when I was literary editor of the *Irish Press* and running the Hennessy Awards, I got him to be one of the judges one year. Then I remember one afternoon in the summer of 1975 I was sitting in my office and there was a ring from reception to say there was a Mr Saroyan to see me. I said, 'You must be joking!' But no, he had been in Scotland and he decided to fly over for a day to come and see me and get to know me. We had a most marvellous day together because the energy of that man and his enthusiasm for life; it was like sitting beside a vase of adrenalin. He came home with me and we had a meal together and he took that Penguin of *The Daring Young Man* and he wrote a lovely long inscription in it.

Growing up in Cork and being interested in the short story, you couldn't but have been influenced by Frank O'Connor, Sean O'Faolain and their mentor, Daniel Corkery. Your copy of Frank O'Connor's collection 'Guests of the Nation' is well read.

O'Connor was a pet man. I met him when I was in my early teens. How I came to meet him was that a mutual friend of mine, who knew that I had been writing poetry and translating from the Irish, showed O'Connor a translation I had done of *An Bannán Buí: The Yellow Bittern*. O'Connor had me along to meet him and as always he gave great praise and was very helpful. 'I'll tell you what you'll do with that translation now,' he said, 'Take it up to Jack White, Literary Editor of *The Irish Times* and tell him I said he's to publish it.' So in those days I had no nerves, it didn't worry me. I went straight up to *the Irish Times*, went in to see Jack White, gave him the poem and said, 'Frank O'Connor says you're to publish this.' I left it with him and waited for two months but nothing happened. I bumped into O'Connor again and he asked, 'Did you ever get that poem published?' When I said I hadn't he said, 'Don't be messing around. Go back up to White and say he must publish it.' So I went back up to Jack White and he said he liked the poem, but it was too long for *The Irish Times*. He asked if he could drop a verse and I agreed and he published it. It was the first time I ever appeared in print. Of course, the catch is O'Connor, White and myself were all from Cork, so it was obviously a mafia event!

Here are some very interesting pamphlets by Eric Cross, who is best known for 'The Tailor and Ansty'. These four pamphlets are called 'Maps of Time'.

These pamphlets, or maps when you open them up, have the lines of longitude as the centuries divided into periods of ten years and the lines of latitude are merely each country in the world. The four of them run from AD 400 to modern times. At a glance you have a whole chronology of world history, and it's so fascinating to pick out a particular year and look down and see what was happening in that year in every country in the world. Eric Cross was, undoubtedly, an unacknowledged genius.

Here's a widely acknowledged genius – Samuel Beckett. The volume we're looking at is an early one of his, 'More Pricks than Kicks'.

It was his only collection of short stories, first published in 1934, and I read it again when I was in my teens. When I started *Irish Writing* in 1945 I wrote to Samuel Beckett and asked him if he would contribute to the magazine. At that time he was completely unknown, although the short stories had been published. He had been forgotten and was living in Paris helping Joyce. He sent me an extract from the novel he was writing at the time and later he sent me another extract. Then years later when I was living in London I was listening on the Third Programme to a talk given by a playwright and he was explaining how all the early plays he wrote were absolutely useless. Then one day on a railway-station bookstall he saw a magazine called *Irish Writing* and he picked it up and opened it and saw something by a man called Samuel Beckett, of whom he had never heard. He read this amazing piece of writing and his whole attitude changed and his whole use of words changed as a result and he scrapped all his plays and wrote new ones and since then he never looked back. That playwright was Harold Pinter. When I heard that I levitated about three feet off the floor, to feel this connection that something I had done had helped Harold Pinter.

19

GERALD DAVIS

Gerald Davis is an artist and proprietor of the Davis Gallery in Dublin which in 1995 celebrated twenty-five years showing the work of some of Ireland's most exciting painters and sculptors. He is also an impresario, jazz connoisseur and record producer whose record label, Livia, recorded Louis Stewart, Brendan Kennelly and Niall Toibín. He is fascinated by the writing of James Joyce and has masqueraded as Leopold Bloom around the world. In 1982, the year of the Joyce Centenary, he embarked on a series of Paintings for Bloomsday which were subsequently published, with text chosen by Terence Brown, under the title *The Joycean Year*. He is a critic and frequent broadcaster on such diverse topics as poetry, Jewish humour and his worldwide travels.

We're in Capel Street in Dublin over the Davis Gallery, home of Gerald Davis, artist, impresario, Joycean and man about town. There are books here on your shelves going back to your schooldays.

I'm afraid I'm a bit of a book addict. I'm a book junkie, in fact, and it's very dangerous for me to go into a bookshop. I've collected books all my life. I don't think I could live without them. The very first book I was given by my parents was *Uncle Tom's Cabin* by Harriet Beecher Stowe and I still have my school copy of Kenneth Grahame's *The Wind in the Willows*. I grew up on *The Wind in the Willows*: it's a gorgeous book and I love it.

You have a lot of books by Irish writers, including a huge section by and about James Joyce. You have even impersonated Leopold Bloom from 'Ulysses'.

I can't honestly say I've read *Ulysses* from start to finish diligently because it takes a lot of effort to do that, but I have experienced the book in many ways. I've had the pleasure of working on it with David Norris, Brendan Kennelly and Terence Brown. I also have a complete set of the tapes of

Willie Styles's wonderful RTE radio dramatisation of *Ulysses*, which is the most comfortable way of experiencing the book. *Ulysses* means a lot to me, and I have tried to embody the spirit of Leopold Bloom on the streets of Dublin and as far away as Sydney in Australia.

Another bible of yours is 'The Best of Myles' by Myles na Gopaleen, whose humour particularly appeals to you.

Well, it has to be for anyone from Dublin. Myles was a direct descendant of Joyce in pulling words apart, and I love his Catechism of Cliché where he satirises common sayings. There's one great one where he talks about what they'll all say about you when you're dead, all the clichés that are trotted out.

> Of what was any deceased citizen you like to mention typical?
> *Of all that is best in Irish life.*
> Correct. With what qualities did he endear himself to all who knew him?
> *His charm of manner and unfailing kindness.*
> Yes. But with what particularly did he impress all those he came into contact with?
> *His sterling quality of mind, loftiness of intellect and unswerving devotion to the national cause.*
> What article of his was always at the disposal of the national language?
> *His purse.*
> And what abstract assistance was readily offered to those who sought it?
> *The fruit of his wide reading and profound erudition.*
> At what time did he speak Irish?
> *At a time when it was neither profitable nor popular.*

That's still as funny today as when it was written fifty years ago, and it has become part of our language.

You mentioned Brendan Kennelly earlier, and you must have everything he ever wrote on your shelves.

I have all of Brendan's books. I love dipping into Brendan's work and I love him dearly. There's one particular poem that means a lot to me and it's about vulnerability. It's the title poem from his collection *Good Souls to Survive*.

Things inside things endure
Longer than things exposed;
We see because we are blind
And should not be surprised to find
We survive because we're enclosed.

If merit is measured at all,
Vulnerability is the measure;
The little desire protection
With something approaching passion,
Will not be injured, cannot face error.

So the bird in astonishing flight
Chokes on the stricken blood,
The bull in the dust is one
With surrendered flesh and bone,
Naked on chill wood.

The real is rightly intolerable,
Its countenance stark and abrupt,
Good souls, to survive, select
Their symbols from among the elect –
Articulate, suave, corrupt.

But from corruption comes the deep
Desire to plunge to the true;
To dare is to redeem the blood,
Discover the buried good,
Be vulnerably new.

I see an American novel by Tom Robbins called 'Skinny Legs and All', which the blurb says is about an Arab and a Jew who open a restaurant together across the road from the United Nations in New York. It sounds like the beginning of a joke.

Tom Robbins is an outrageous writer. I first discovered him with *Even Cowgirls Get the Blues* and I just saw his name on this book, knew nothing about it and was totally entranced by it. It is an hilariously funny book. I think he is a very important writer because his metaphors are absolutely incredible. He just blasts you all the time. He also has an awful lot to say about philosophy, religion, art and meaning. In this passage he satirises the modern conceptual art movement. This gallery dealer finds this guy who has made a gigantic silver turkey out of a mobile home and she sells it to the Museum of Modern Art as a wonderful art piece. She wants him to produce more and here she is talking to this artist:

> What I find in your pictures finally is an awkward dichotomy between illusion and abstraction. Energetic, yes. Charming, yes. But as I said, awkward. They typify the unloving nuttiness of modern art before it finally matured and developed a social conscience. What are you saying with your enormous silver turkey, Mr Boomer? It seems fraught, simply fraught, with commentary.

It's a wonderful send up of the gobbledegook of a lot of modern art criticism.

As one might expect from an artist, you have a lot of beautifully illustrated art books from all periods on your shelves.

I've been very lucky because I've built up this collection since I was a child. When I went to St Andrew's College there was an art teacher there called Chris Ryan and he encouraged us to buy little books from Parsons' Bookshops for half a crown each, and I still have them. They were terrific little collections of the work of Van Gogh, Lautrec, Picasso, and since then I've been collecting art books.

Samuel Beckett is a writer you greatly admire, and I see his novel 'Malone Dies' on your shelves.

I have loved Beckett since I saw *Waiting for Godot* in the Pike Theatre when I was sixteen years old. I've dipped into his novels. I love this passage from *Malone Dies* where the man is lying dead. It is full of vindictiveness.

> I shall soon be quite dead at last in spite of all. Perhaps next month. Then it will be the month of April or of May. For the year is still young, a thousand little signs tell me so. Perhaps I am wrong, perhaps I shall survive Saint John the Baptist's Day and even the Fourteenth of July, festival of freedom. Indeed I would not put it past me to pant on to the Transfiguration, not to speak of the Assumption. But I do not think so, I do not think I am wrong in saying that these rejoicings will take place in my absence, this year… Let me say before I go any further that I forgive nobody. I wish them all an atrocious life and then the fires and ice of hell and in the execrable generations to come an honoured name.

I see here a volume I can't pass. It's called 'The Art of Sexual Ecstasy' and you didn't bother to hide it.

I've had a healthy interest in all sorts of sexual books since I was a kid. In fact I think I'm quite an expert on pornography at this stage! I got this book in the post from Aquarian Books for review. It's by Margot Anand and it's subtitled 'The Path of Sacred Sex and Sexuality for Western Lovers.' One of my favourite books on sex is Alex Comfort's *The Joy of Sex* which is a wonderful manual for lovers. This other book is at a different level. It's a metaphysical approach to the whole sexual thing, which I don't mind having a look at.

I have strong views about censorship and pornography. I don't like censorship at all. I now find that in my mid-fifties I'm getting quite reactionary and an awful lot of what I see in the cinema I find quite appalling. At the same time I don't believe in censoring it, but I believe we should educate ourselves and our children to be able to sort out that which is good from the bad. I don't think there is such a thing as obscenity in art. There's obscenity in anti-art and there's obscenity in ugliness and there's obscenity in war. There is no obscenity in true art.

20

HELEN LUCY BURKE

Helen Lucy Burke wears many varied hats: novelist, short-story writer, journalist, theatre critic and restaurant reviewer. She was born in Dublin and in a previous existence worked in local government. Her writing is marked by a caustic wit and an incisive analysis of Irish life. Her novel *Close Connections* (1979), which has been compared to *The Ginger Man*, explores hilariously the clash of sex and sanctity in the new Ireland. Her collection of short stories, *A Season for Mothers* (1980), depicts the resentments and traps of family relationships and the paradoxical pull between the old and new moralities in contemporary Ireland.

Helen Lucy Burke, when we look at your bookshelves, we see an enormous number of books by Patrick O'Brien. He is a writer on whose behalf you've been crusading for some time now.

For a number of years I was telling people how wonderful Patrick O'Brien was and they used look at me with amazement on their faces. Now he has taken off: he's like a bush fire that sweeps the landscape. He is now big money in America and is one of the twentieth century's most wonderful novelists – he has been compared, not improbably, with Proust. I myself would read him in preference to Proust. He is not just a writer of sea sagas. The one I'm re-reading at the moment is *Thirteen Gun Salute* which is set off the coast of Java. His saga treats of the adventures of an English captain during the naval command of Lord Nelson and his great friend, who is an Irish doctor and spy called Stephen Maturin. Maturin is a self-portrait of the author: he is multilingual, interested in flowers and interested in birds. It explores the very unlikely friendship of these two different men, and it is a beautiful friendship because it is between this English captain and Irish doctor who love each other solidly without the slightest element of homosexuality. This is a friendship and a love without any other tinge: they both have female loves as well. In this sixteen volume saga there are characters who are introduced then drop out. They live their separate lives. Things happen to these characters and the two central people change as the saga goes on. Experience changes them. I would not part with one of Patrick O'Brien's novels for diamonds.

Moving along your shelves I see you have Henry Fielding's two volume novel 'Tom Jones', a great comic picaresque eighteenth-century novel.

I keep those volumes convenient to me because every year I re-read *Tom Jones*. I don't just read the action parts but also the introductions to each section, which are very funny indeed. They are very satiric and very funny. Henry Fielding was a wonderful life-enhancing author. In fact I have Fielding's take-off of his contemporary Samuel Richardson's novel *Pamela*, which he called *An Apology for the Life of Miss Shamela Andrews*, in which Richardson's heroine was exposed for the prurient and noxious little whore that she was. He is a great author and I wish he had written more. Another great eighteenth-century novel, in the epistolary mode, is Pierre Choderlos de Laclos' *Les Liaisons Dangereuses*. I read it in French because you can appreciate the style better in the original language. The letters in this novel are not straining at the seams but each one has a valid reason for existing. This is a reasonable and logical book and also one of the most subversive books you will ever read. It is a chronicle of evil, coldly plotted, and the fact that it is sexual evil makes no whit of difference. It is a saga of power and manipulation. I don't think Christopher Hampton's stage version captured the evil spirit of the novel. In fact, I had a great discussion with the actor Alan Stanford, who appeared in it at the Gate Theatre. We kept screaming at each other the episodes we would like to have seen in the stage version which were left out. Hampton's stage version is an honourable attempt, but a television serial might have been more effective.

You like diaries and letters, and you have a beautiful edition of 'The Memories of John Evelyn, Esq.' comprising his diaries from 1614–1705 and a selection of his letters.

Evelyn was a superb diarist who held various positions of importance in the civil service of King Charles I, Charles II and James II. He saw everything at first hand. He gives a marvellous portrait of Nell Gwyn, whom he violently disapproved of. He experienced at first hand the Popish Plot and the Titus Oates conspiracy. He was even present when Titus Oates was whipped and pilloried:

> Oates who had but two days before been pilloried at several places and whipped at the cart's tail from Newgate to Aldgate was this day placed on a sledge, being not able by reason of so late scourging, and dragged from prison to Tyburn and whipped again all the way which some thought to be very severe and extraordinary. But if he was guilty of the perjuries and so of the death of many innocents, as I fear he was, his punishment was but what he deserved. I chanced to pass just as execution was doing on him, a strange revolution.

I've worked it out. It meant about six or seven miles of constant whipping which is a fairly severe punishment. It beats hollow the six strokes of the birch administered in Singapore for vandalising a car. With Evelyn you get the different swings of his opinion as events happen. You get a close-up of William of Orange's marriage to Princess Mary and King Charles II, and his favourites. He was present at all these historical events and his diaries make marvellous reading.

You are a great fan of poetry of the great classical age, and Alexander Pope is a particular favourite of yours.

My own favourite all-purpose quotation is from Pope:

> Yes, I am proud and must be proud to see
> Men not afraid of God afraid of me.

I don't really feel like that but it is a nice thing to say. I love Pope because he is witty and elegant and he had a greater command of the English language than nearly anybody I've ever come across. He used language like a rapier rather than like a broadsword. He darted his point into the heart. We need a man like that around nowadays.

I love the modern poets as well, and I regard Paul Durcan as being something in that line of succession from Pope – I love Durcan's manic use of language and his weird view of events. It's just as correct to describe a landscape when you are standing on your head as when you are standing on your feet. Durcan gives you a different eyeview. I often wish that Paul Durcan would start writing short stories – if he did he would be one of the world's great masters.

Wearing another hat, as a restaurant critic you enjoy books about food. I see here a volume called 'Seafood: A Connoisseur's Guide and Cookbook' by Alan Davison and Charlotte Knox, with beautiful illustrations.

This volume was given to me by the author himself, Alan Davison, who was British Ambassador to Laos. He left the diplomatic service after writing a novel under an assumed name which revealed secrets of the diplomatic life. These illustrations make a herring look superbly beautiful, on a par with a painting by Titian. It captures the individuality of the fish: whether its flesh is firm or close and how you should treat it. Look at the illustrations of lobsters and shrimps: each one is a poem in colour. Who wouldn't want to cook a halibut with its two eyes looking sideways out of its head? Look at the surprised censorious expression on the face of the turbot. This swordfish has round yellow eyes like something from a box of sweets, and these needles are the eels and elvers. I almost, at this stage, prefer reading about food to eating it. I'm like a musician who reads the score of Beethoven, because you get the ideal music from reading the score and you get the ideal meal from reading the recipe book.

21

SISTER STANISLAUS KENNEDY

Sister Stanislaus Kennedy is the Director of Focus Point for homeless people. She was born in County Kerry and educated locally and at University College, Dublin and the University of Manchester. A member of the Irish Sisters of Charity, she has devoted her life to looking after the underprivileged in society. She was involved in the Kilkenny Social Services from 1969 to 1982, carried out research on the needs of homeless women in Dublin and established the Focus Housing Association to help homeless people find and maintain a home. She has been conferred with an Honorary Doctorate from Trinity College and honoured with various awards and titles, including Person of the Year. Her publications include *One Million Poor, But Where Shall I Go?* and *Streetwise Children Out-of-Home.*

Sister Stanislaus Kennedy, the first book I see on your shelves is Brian Keenan's 'An Evil Cradling' which, in a way, is an account of a spiritual journey.

I think this is a magnificent book because it really is about the struggle with himself, that whole inward journey. Coming out of what could have been a devastating experience, Brian Keenan discovered an almost indestructible strength within himself. I found that quite extraordinary, quite exciting but also quite inspiring. What I linked that experience with really was Primo Levi's books, in the sense that Levi was writing very much in the same vein after being in the concentration camps. His books *If This Is Man* and *Moments of Reprieve* are most extraordinary where over and over again, he talks about what gave him strength and how he gave strength to other people. The discipline of showering every day and an older man encouraging him, he says, kept his spirit strong and gave him an inner strength that nobody could destroy. Brian Keenan reminded me very much of Primo Levi in his struggle with self and [in] his inner strength. I think these two men drew their inspiration from an inner strength of the spirit that's in everybody if we draw on it. If I look at it as a Christian I would say it's the spirit – not the psyche, but that deeper part of the self that is the spirit. People call it different things. It doesn't matter what you call it but it is important that people know that it is there and that when we find ourselves in darkness, or indeed discover our own darkness, that the spirit is strong enough to bring us out of the darkness. What is important to remember is that central core of our being is spirit. It is the place that God touches. Now we might not believe in God. We might say it is the power of the universe, but it is an inner strength.

I notice a lot of the books on your shelves are in that cross-over area between spirituality and psychology and science. You are obviously fascinated by how spirituality enters into other areas of modern life.

We are drawn to books by something inside ourselves, books that reflect what we are looking for ourselves or where we are ourselves. What strikes me is that all my readings are around that inner struggle, around light and darkness. This book here, *The Conjectures of a Guilty Bystander* by Thomas Merton, is written by an extraordinary man who led an extraordinary life. Having become a contemplative monk he moved out of the world, one would say, but in fact he didn't. This book is simply the conjectures of a bystander who was looking at life. In it he refers to Camus, Gandhi, Bonhoeffer, de Chardin, and he has a comment on them all. He talks about himself being part of the world, and he says very clearly in one extract here:

> In Louisville, at the corner of Fourth and Walnut, in the centre of a shopping district, I was suddenly overwhelmed with the realisation that I loved all of these people, that they were mine and I theirs, that we could not be alien to one another even though we were total strangers.

Merton is absolutely rooted in the world because he is rooted in God. He has that wonderful sense of being able to comment on everything, and that really appeals to me.

Here's a volume called 'Care of the Soul' by Thomas Moore, subtitled 'How to Add Depth and Meaning to Your Everyday Life'.

Thomas Moore was a Cistercian monk who left and became a Jungian psychologist. What he does here is something that many writers do not do: he links psychology and spirituality. Psychology is very much about the psyche. He links them in a very ordinary way and he talks about very ordinary things in life. I think it's a great book for anybody interested in care of the soul, in finding a greater depth and meaning in their life. It's written in a simple style where you wouldn't really think you were reading spirituality or psychology, but in fact you are reading both.

Even when you are reading contemporary fiction I suspect you are looking for writers who have something profound to say. One of the writers I know you admire greatly is Brian Moore. I see here on your shelves 'The Lonely Passion of Judith Hearne' and 'I Am Mary Dunne'. What's so special for you about Brian Moore?

I think he sees beyond the ordinary. He sees the profound in the ordinary, but he also sees that whole depth of the soul. He sees in women their sadness, their oppression, in a way that not many other authors do. I suppose it's the whole humanity of it that appeals to me. He crosses all the boundaries and can write about most things, because I think Brian Moore understands about life and he understands about human nature. He also makes a connection between the inside and the outside. He grasps the human struggle in a great way and he grasps that sadness of life too. *Black Robe* I thought was a brilliant book. His understanding there of all the characters and what was going on inside them is most impressive. He can describe them with a beauty that draws you in to him. I think he is very profound. What he is able to do is focus in on people at a time of crisis in their lives and bring it to us in a way that we can understand it. He can explore that crisis with great depth because he is obviously a person of great insight himself. You can't do that unless you have a great knowledge of self, and it's that knowledge of self that leads you into that.

I see you have a number of volumes of poetry on your shelves, including 'Lifelines', that wonderful anthology of poems chosen by famous people, compiled by the students of Wesley College and edited by Niall McMonagle. What did you choose for that anthology yourself?

I chose a poem by Patrick Kavanagh called 'Street Corner Christ'. We tend to choose the things that reflect our own lives. We look for things in books, or they hit us in a very strong way. That poem by Kavanagh is a very simple poem in which he saw Christ in the tattered beggarman on the side of the street. I love Kavanagh – he is so earthy, so rural, yet so spiritual. He cuts right through everything. That poem of his, 'Stony Grey Soil' is very fine; he is very conscious of how the harsh life of rural Ireland took away his freedom. Yet at the end of that poem he talks about how it gave him a strength and a vision to go on. I often quote his line 'Don't mind the men on the Brady's Hill', because if you were to mind the men on Brady's Hill you wouldn't ever do much. He gives ordinary things a very special meaning. I suppose that is the gift of the poet really, to make us think and think again. What Kavanagh was able to see was reality. We don't see reality at all. We see pieces of reality, the pieces we want to see.

I think Brendan Kennelly also does that. It's his ability to force us to look at reality. I think he has a big thing about celebration, celebration of darkness. In the preface to his earlier poem he talks about how blind he can be. He says:

> I believe each of us is blind in a great number of ways that saves us. I believe that occasionally we see things in our blindness and that elevates us. We are cripplingly limited. To recognise this is a strength. To celebrate it is to discover a kind of indestructibility, to achieve definition, to be purified.

I think that's tremendous. That is what the poet can do for us. Poets help us to be able to celebrate our darkness. In the world today we run away from our darkness, yet our darkness is light just as our weakness is our strength. Our inner strength comes from facing that darkness within us.

I also think that T. S. Eliot is a wonderful poet. I would pick up *The Selected Poems of T. S. Eliot* any time and read. His poetry is simple yet profound. It's like reading the Bible. Every line has a meaning and it's full of mystery. In *Four Quartets* he has a line:

> But perhaps neither gain nor loss
> For us there is only the trying
> The rest is not our business.

To really live in the now and celebrate the now is all we are asked to do. The rest will work itself out.

22

JOHN A. MURPHY

John A. Murphy, who was born in Macroom, County Cork, was Professor of Irish History at University College, Cork and served as a Senator representing the National University of Ireland. He taught on the staff of St Finbarr's College in Cork from 1949 to 1960, before becoming lecturer and later Professor of Irish History at UCC. He has had a lifelong interest in contemporary Irish politics, history, archaeology, music and the Irish language. His publications include *Ireland in the Twentieth Century* and *De Valera and His Times*, which he co-edited with J. P. O'Carroll. He has been a frequent broadcaster and controversial columnist in the Irish media.

We're in University College Cork in what might rather grandiosely be described as the retirement home of Professor and Senator John A. Murphy, where you soldiered in the History Department for over thirty years.

Since 1960 indeed, and I was Professor of History from 1971 to 1990. This is what you might call my Granny Office, and I'm very pleased to be here, except of course it's not nearly big enough to accommodate my books. One of my favourite books, which some of my friends will be intrigued to hear, is a copy of the Bible. It was a book which was given to my mother on the day of her wedding by a first cousin of my father, who was in fact the priest who married them, Archdeacon Cullinane. So, for that reason alone it is very precious to me. I have always been fascinated by the Old Testament, because I can't make sense of a lot of it and I ignore all the little pious footnotes telling me what I should think about it. I have always been fascinated since boyhood by the stories in the Old Testament. I remember, as a small boy, being so enthralled by the story of David and his son Absalom, who rebelled against him, but his father didn't want to see him killed. He was, nonetheless, killed and David's grief so impressed me as a child that I used to go around the house pretending to weep and crying out, 'My son, Absalom! Absalom, my son! Would to God I might die for thee, Absalom, my son. My son, Absalom!' Eventually, my mother told me to shut up, fearing what the neighbours might think. I've been intrigued by that and many other stories in the Bible and that copy, with its associations, is very important to me.

Another book which has been a constant companion of yours is 'Dinneen's Irish-English Dictionary', a veritable treasurehouse of language.

My wife gave me a copy of this in 1971 when it could be bought for a few shillings. What I like about it is that it is in the Cló-Ghaelach, with the Irish words in the Gaelic print. We've become so used to the modern script we forget how beautiful the old Gaelic script was. Above all it's the rather eccentric but very learned content of the book that fascinates me. You remember Myles na Gopaleen used to make great fun of Dinneen, allegedly quoting definitions where the one word, he claimed, was defined as 'a rare disease in sheep' and 'a loud sound made in an empty house by an unauthorised person'. That joke is close enough to the actual reality. There's always something to intrigue, and whenever you open it you find a gem. For example, yesterday I found this word *coimhirse* and it means 'friendliness, camaraderie and reconciliation' and he goes on to illustrate it with a sentence: *'Tabhair dom coimhise is cur píopa dearg im' láimh'* or 'Give me your friendship and put a lighted pipe in my hand'. Dinneen then goes on to explain that to smoke the same pipe was a sign of friendship, and the custom was widespread among Irish regiments in the British army. That kind of information offered in such a casual fashion is part of the attraction of that great book.

From the many hundreds of volumes on Irish history on your shelves you have picked out J. C. Beckett's 'The Anglo-Irish Tradition'.

What attracts me above all to books on history like Beckett's is that they are well written. He has a lovely elegant style. This book deals with the Anglo-Irish in all its complications and wide definitions – cultural, political, social, religious. I'm fascinated by the Anglo-Irish tradition in Ireland, fascinated as much by what it could have done as by what it achieved. My own feeling is that the Anglo-Irish missed their chance at a number of points of creating a real brotherhood of Irishmen in this country. It wasn't the fault of all of them: for example, Beckett has a very shrewd assessment of Thomas Davis in this book. Of Davis he says, 'This attractive, romantic, able but ineffective young man stands, not inappropriately, as the symbol of something that has never existed: a truly non-sectarian Irish nationalism.' This book is an elegy for part of the fabric of the Irish heritage that is no longer with us really, in any real sense.

Another cherished volume of history on your shelves is Joe Lee's 'Ireland 1912–1985: Politics and Society', written by a fellow historian and colleague of yours.

The connection is closer than that insofar as my own book *Ireland in the Twentieth Century* was published in 1975 covering much the same period. My volume was much slimmer and I suppose I envy Joe Lee's ability to write in the same area at such great length. Joe Lee would want to watch the tendency to be regarded as a guru, in that everywhere you see him quoted with some comment on contemporary Irish society. That's understandable in a way, because in this book you get the impression he is in a hurry to get to the extended sermon at the end of the book which everyone always dips into. The great body of the book is brilliantly written twentieth century Irish history. It's a book into which I would constantly dip for that reason.

Leon O Broin was a remarkable twentieth century Irishman and you have here his autobiography, 'Just Like Yesterday'. Why does he appeal to you?

First of all he belongs to a class of writer who can evoke a period so vividly. In the case of Leon O Broin he was both a participant in the 1916 Revolution and went on to become a distinguished public servant and in his retirement a most prolific historian. He writes superbly, with great humanity and with great humour. Among other things he recalls the time when he and his wife were living in Baltinglass and he heard a great story about a local woman, Mrs Hayden, who looked after the church so well that nothing connected with it could happen without her. A little child was being taken round the Stations of the Cross one day by her mother and at the Twelfth Station it suddenly dawned on her that the good Jesus had been killed. 'Who killed him?' she said amazed. 'The Jews,' her mother told her. 'The Jews?' said the youngster. 'And where was Mrs Hayden?'

Moving away from more formal history to literary history and anecdotal reminiscences, I see you have on your shelves John Ryan's 'Remembering How We Stood', an ironic title I often think, considering so many of the Irish literary subjects he wrote about so often staggered or were busy falling down.

I suppose in every sensible man – and I would regard myself by and large as being sensible – there is a hankering to do something really wild. I have a vicarious urge to be part of that world of Brendan Behan, Patrick Kavanagh, Myles na Gopaleen and company. John Ryan recalls those days very well, simply and innocently. Anthony Cronin has also recalled those days very well in his book *Dead as Doornails* and in his biography of Myles, *No Laughing Matter*. John Ryan was able to stand apart from all these people and observe them as we would, so it makes for a fascinating read. Ryan is more benign about these Dublin literati than Cronin, who is more clinical, although he was part of them himself. Hugh Leonard in his autobiographical volumes *Home Before Night* and *Out After Dark* is also a superb and transparent stylist. The depiction of his parents and, in particular, his relationship with his father are most moving and touching.

You have a particular interest in poetry and song in the Irish language, and I see here the Dolmen Press anthology. 'An Duanaire: 1600–1990: Poems of the Dispossessed', edited by Sean Ó Tuama and Thomas Kinsella.

I will always recall before publication of this book the public performances of Sean Ó Tuama reciting the Irish-language originals with Thomas Kinsella's sparse bleak translations. Those were performances to be remembered, and that is what this book means to me. I think, above all, this anthology illustrates how our ancestors resisted oppression, not perhaps in the conventional sense of nationalists fighting the British Empire, but rather standing up to their class oppressors. There is something quintessentially

Irish about Seán Clárach Mac Dónaill's eighteenth-century famous poem on Dawson, a Tipperary landlord who was much detested:

> Taiscidh, a chlocha, fa choigilt i gcormead criadh
> An feallaire fola 's an stollaire, Dawson liath.

> *Keep fast under cover, o stones, in closet of clay*
> *This grey-haired Dawson, a bloody and treacherous butcher.*

There is something very elemental about that which appeals to me, a recognition of the power of the poet to immortalise or damn forever the subject of his poem in a few pithy lines.

23

ITA DALY

Ita Daly was born in County Leitrim but her family moved to Dublin when she was thirteen and she was educated at St Louis High School in Rathmines and University College, Dublin where she took a degree in English and Spanish. She taught for eleven years until the birth of her daughter in 1979. Her first collection of short stories, *The Lady with the Red Shoes*, was highly acclaimed, and her stories won two Hennessy Literary Awards and *The Irish Times* Short Story Competition. Her subsequent fiction includes *Ellen*, *A Singular Attraction*, *Dangerous Fictions* and a children's book, *Candy on the Dart*. Her stories have appeared in Irish, British and American anthologies and her novels have been translated into German, Swedish and Danish. She is married to the writer David Marcus.

Ita Daly, the first book I see here on your shelves is 'The Poolbeg Anthology of Elizabeth Bowen's Irish Stories'. She's a writer you admire greatly.

She's one of my favourite writers and I absolutely love all her work, her novels and her short stories. She's a wonderful stylist, the kind of prose writer you have to read very slowly, savouring her sentences and examining the way she uses language. I particularly like this book Poolbeg Press brought out in the late '70s. There is something very special in the way Elizabeth Bowen deals with the Irish language. She has a way of catching the essence of Irish landscapes and Irish country distances and towns which means that, although most of the stories in this collection were written and published in the '40s, they haven't dated in the way a lesser writer might. If you read some stories a lot of the descriptions are mere lists – you go to a town and the writer talks about the bookshop and the fish shop and the pizzeria. Elizabeth Bowen, in her descriptions, gets to the truth of things, she gets to something that is constant. In one of her stories, called 'Summer Journey', she is driving through Cork, and every time I go over the border into that county I think of that story and the hairs of the back of my head stand up because I'm there with her. It's about a married woman travelling through the night to meet her illicit lover and she calls in at a little country hotel to make a phone call. The whole story is so real and so living fifty years after it was written. This is the mark of a truly great writer, whom I believe Elizabeth Bowen to be. I wouldn't put myself as a writer, in the same category as Elizabeth Bowen but I wish I could write a tenth as well as she does.

Another book about a very interesting woman is this biography of Rosa Luxembourg, the great 'European Socialist'.

Rosa Luxembourg is one of my heroines, a huge character striding across European socialism. This biography is by a German woman called Elizabeth Ettinger and it deals with her as a revolutionary. She was a great socialist who founded the first Marxist party in Poland and was a prominent member of the Second International. She was very influential in socialist thought right through the early years of the century. She was three times an outcast – first as a Jew, second as a woman and third as a cripple. She let none of this influence her but she kicked over the traces. She lost her faith very early and became an atheist. She left her home, went to university in Switzerland, joined the Communist Party at a very early stage and met and fell in love with a Russian revolutionary with whom she lived for years. Towards the end of her life she met another man years younger than her. Then in 1919 she was assassinated in Germany and died in a ditch. What I love about this book is not so much the vivid details it gives about her life as a revolutionary, but the way it brings alive this woman of huge passions. She was a superwoman before the term was coined, because she wanted everything. She wanted to be a revolutionary and to change the process of European thought, but she also wanted to have a husband and children and a home. Right to the end of her life this great revolutionary figure was looking for love in her life. She said that love transforms life, changes it from the mundane into something like a fairytale.

A far cry from the world of international politics is a little Penguin book in a series called 'English Cooking: Ancient and Modern', and this one by Elizabeth Davis is called 'Spice, Salt and the Aromatics in the English Kitchen'.

I think a lot of the books Elizabeth Davis has written about the food of France and Italy are dull, but I think this little book is an exception. Here she includes a lot of recipes which are not her own, from the sixteenth to the nineteenth centuries. It's not just a recipe book but a history of English and Anglo-Indian societies over the centuries. It's full of little glimpses into the kitchen of Anglo-Indian colonels and people like that. It's also full of the most interesting recipes including this one from Dorset in the eighteenth century on How to Dry a Goose:

> Take the fairest and fattest goose you can get, dry him well within, take out the soul. Then take some bay salt and heat it well and let him lie a fortnight in salt. Then tie him up in paper and hang him up in a chimney where they burn wood or coal. Let him hang a fortnight or three weeks and in that time he will be ready to boil. You may keep him longer, if you please, before you boil him.

Kate O'Brien was a woman who fell in love with Spain, and I know you have had a love affair with Spain too and with Spanish literature. You have the Virago Edition of Kate O'Brien's 'Farewell Spain' prominently on your shelves.

I think Kate O'Brien is a very important Irish writer who, I am glad to say, is far less neglected than she used to be. I love her novels, but this book, *Farewell Spain*, is a sort of elegiac travel book. She went to Spain as a *señorita* in her twenties to mind children and thus began a lifelong love affair with Spain. This book was written at the beginning of the Spanish Civil War when she knew that Spain would be irrevocably changed. Although she stayed in Spain she wasn't a Communist but had great sympathy with the Republic, and she thought that the Republic should be given a chance to flex its muscles and see what it could do. She also had no time for Franco or the colonels, and significantly the book was banned in Spain. She was prevented from returning to Spain until 1957. The book shows us what an excellent travel writer she is and it also shows what a wonderfully sane and balanced woman she is. All good travel writing is as much about the writer as the places they visit, and Kate O'Brien is very much present in this book as a personality. She also understands something fundamental about Spain which a lot of people miss: it's not a happy colourful Mediterranean society and culture. It is a very dark, melancholic culture, and she captures that in this book, *Farewell Spain*.

Another great travel writer you like is Dervla Murphy, and you have her autobiography, 'Wheels Within Wheels'. Interesting that she too, in common with other writers on your shelves, is a very strong woman who has led an extraordinarily unconventional life.

I didn't realise that all the books I have spoken about so far have been either by or about women. I admire all of them because, firstly, they have all achieved something, and, secondly, they are all women of great talent. I have been fascinated by Dervla Murphy for years since I read her first book about cycling to India. I admire her as one of the greatest contemporary travel writers but I choose her autobiography, *Wheels Within Wheels*, because I wondered what makes her tick. What on earth made her, when in her early twenties, get up and leave her little sleepy town of Lismore in the Blackwater Valley and get on her bicycle and set off to cycle to India? I think I found part of the secret because in this autobiography she deals with her childhood when her mother was an invalid and her father was a local librarian in Lismore. Dervla was an only child. What you notice is how clear-headed and clear-sighted she is about the muddle of family life in those early years. She looks very objectively at her situation. She can see her parents for what they are and she sees herself for what she is. She loves her parents, but she knows that above and beyond anything else she wants to be a a writer, even if it means getting up and making the break from an invalid mother. She has the kind of toughness which all good travel writers must have, and she is also as individualistic as Kate O'Brien or Rosa Luxembourg or Elizabeth Bowen.

Your next book, 'The Diaries of Evelyn Waugh', is by a very different writer and man of the world.

I'm very attracted to Evelyn Waugh. I think simply because of his madness. He seems to me to be such an extraordinary person. I think he is a very important writer and I like his work. I think he is a savage satirist and I read and re-read his novels with great satisfaction. Who could resist the diaries of this absolute looney? They go from the time he was a public schoolboy in Lancing right through the '20s, '30s, '40s and up to the '60s. A lot of diaries read as if they were written for publication but not these, because you don't get that whiff off them. I think Waugh was simply too mad to worry about publication. He had not got the conventional faults of human beings: all his faults are huge. For example, he actively disliked his children and talks about his son Auberon being clumsy with absolutely no aesthetic or intellectual qualities at all. He talks about one of his daughters having this mincing manner and another as being intensely vain. He tells this really funny story about Lord Longford which encapsulates his gift as a novelist, in that he tells the story and makes no comment on it because he doesn't need to. At one stage Waugh decided he was going to buy a castle in Ireland and this was very peculiar because he hated the Irish and thought they were a race of bogtrotters. Anyway he was coming over to live among us. He told this to various acquaintances in London, among whom was Frank Packenham, later Lord Longford. Packenham threw his hands up in the air and said, 'I must introduce you to people over there. Now you'll have to meet people there. Now who will you have to meet? Of course! De Valera, you must meet Eamon de Valera!' This tells you all you need to know about Packenham, another looney. I was dying to know what made Waugh tick, but at the end of these diaries you haven't got a clue except that he loves to eat, he loves to drink, he smokes too much, he loathes his children and he loathes mankind. He has a great respect for Catholicism and, in a strange way, he continues to believe in a personal God. That's one of the great mysteries about Waugh: how this man who hates everything continues to believe in an all-loving God.

We have time for just a verse of the Spanish poet Lorca, because I know he is a great favourite of yours and you have here 'The Penguin Book of Spanish Verse'. What poem of Lorca have you chosen?

This is a poem called 'Cancíon de jinete', so very typical of Lorca, full of the luminous and the mysterious which typify Lorca's poetry.

Jaca negra, luna grande,	*Small black house and great moon,*
y aceitunas en me alforja.	*And olives in my saddle bag.*
Aunque sepa los caminos	*Although I know the road*
yo nunca llegare a Cordoba.	*I shall never reach Cordoba.*

24

EDWARD DELANEY

Edward Delaney, one of Ireland's most distinguished sculptors, who works mainly in bronze, was educated at the National College of Art in Dublin, the Academy of Fine Art in Munich and the Institute Bella Arte Rosa in Rome. He has exhibited extensively in Ireland and has shown his work abroad in New York, Tokyo, Buenos Aires and Budapest. Among his best known public works in Ireland are the bronze statues of Wolfe Tone and Thomas Davis in Dublin and the works for the ESB and Department of the Environment in Galway and the Connemara Sculpture Park. He is an artist who has broken new ground in Irish sculpture in terms of technique, subject matter and distinctive style. He has won many international awards and is a member of Aosdana.

If you turn off the main road in the centre of Carraroe, County Galway and wind your way through the stone wall landscape, you come upon a remarkable house. This house is distinguished by the huge stainless steel sculptures standing outside it and around it. Then you know you've reached the home of Edward Delaney, sculptor, and we're sitting now in his studio looking out at the Atlantic and surrounded by work in progress and some of his favourite books. The first book I see is 'Brendan Behan's Island: An Irish Sketchbook' by Behan, with drawings by Paul Hogarth. Brendan Behan was a friend of yours.

I'm one of the few people who have never said publicly that Behan was a friend of mine. So many people in Dublin claim to have known Behan. I'd say I knew Behan better than most people. I did Behan a lot of favours. I knew him at the time when he was writing for the *Irish Press* and he was supposed to travel round the country to write articles about local affairs but he never left Dublin! I used to supply him with liquor in the Reading Room of the National Library in Kildare Street where he used to go through the local provincial papers and write an article as if he really was there. If he had the fare to Waterford to write about local events there he'd spend it on drink and never leave Dublin. He couldn't leave the National Library while he was writing the article about Waterford in case he was seen by his fellow *Irish Press* journalists! This book, *Brendan Behan's Island*, is a lovely edition with drawings by Paul Hogarth, including one of my house, because Behan used to come here to Carraroe. This is a drawing of my old house before I did the extension with a man in the foreground on the beach picking seaweed. A lot of people from Carraroe are mentioned in the book, and Behan used to swim down on the beach across the road here. He used to carry young kids piggyback and swim out to sea, which was rather frightening really. He was a wonderfully colourful character who lives in the memory of the people of Carraroe. Hogarth's drawings in this book also have a great feeling for the people and the landscape of Connemara.

Here's an interesting book, beautifully illustrated, 'The Artist and the Pope', and it is based on the personal recollections of Giacomo Manzu who worked as an artist with Pope John XXIII and was commissioned to execute the bronze doors of St Peter's in Rome.

That's an unusual book because I first met Manzu in 1966 in Salzburg and worked with him for two semesters. Manzu worked with a girl I knew who used to model for him and he eventually married her. When I went to Milan four years later I found the same lady in his studio and they had two kids. The saga went on and I worked with him on the casting of the bronze doors for St Peter's in the foundry in Milan, and all those bronze reliefs you see in this book, I was involved in their casting. Manzu had a most amazing relationship with Pope John XXIII because an African Cardinal didn't want an atheist artist doing the doors for St Peter's in Rome. Pope John XXIII said that the artist had been chosen and he couldn't do anything about it. There was a controversy over the depiction of the Assumption of the Blessed Virgin, body and soul into heaven. Mary is depicted as all dressed up for her Assumption into heaven and Manzu said to the Pope, 'How do you know what day Mary was assumed into heaven – did she decide? Maybe she wanted to go racing instead!' The conversations in the book between the Pope and the artist, who both came from the same town in Northern Italy, are fascinating. Manzu had a sad and troubled later life when his kids were kidnapped and he had to pay a ransom. He had a mental breakdown after the kids were returned, but they were kidnapped again and finally he went to live in Switzerland where he died. I wanted to visit him there but I never did because I was told he was in such poor health.

Another book by and about an artist is a volume entitled 'David Smith by David Smith', with text and photographs by the author. You admire Smith very much.

David Smith I consider one of the most powerful if not the most influential American sculptor of the 1960s. His style was never really fully recognised. He worked outside New York but I first met him in Munich and became a very good friend of his. In actual fact I gave him a letter of introduction to the sculptor Henry Moore, and he went to visit Moore. I got a crazy postcard from them signed by two very alcoholic gentlemen.

Smith was eventually killed very tragically in a car accident. Now Smith's work is considered very fashionable. He belonged to the same group as Klein and he drank in the famous New York Cider Bar. During his lifetime he was never popular because he worked in stainless steel and then he painted his sculptures which was rather rare at the time. Smith attacked the American establishment, saying they didn't need sculpture because they put all their bronze into their plumbing and all their marble into their toilets. Consequently they had no need for sculptors.

Another book on your art and craft is 'Bronzes' by Jennifer Montague, a beautifully illustrated volume with colour and black and white photographs.

That book actually is to do with bronzes and I bought it cheaply in the National Gallery in Dublin. It tells, among other things, about the great bronzes which were failures in their casting. One was the famous statue of Frederick of Denmark, 'Man on a Horse'. The king went to look at the casting and suddenly all the metal poured out on to the floor while the king was there and there was uproar. This book is a very fine book which covers the history of bronzes from the earliest Greek times, and the illustrations are superb.

An Irish writer whose death mask you executed was Austin Clarke, and I see you have his 'Selected Poems' prominently on your shelves. You knew Clarke.

I knew Austin Clarke and his family well when they lived in a house in Templeogue which is sadly no longer standing. I used to meet him a lot in Dublin but I met him first in Belfast where he was involved in Mary O'Malley's Lyric Theatre and I was designing sets there for plays by Yeats. Austin Clarke was honoured in Belfast for his work with the Lyric Theatre. Anyhow, to do the death mask I spent a whole day in St Vincent's Hospital surrounded by five or six dead men. Clarke's reputation as a poet has been played down because his publisher, the late Liam Miller of Dolmen who did such wonderful work publishing Irish poets' never had the wide distribution necessary to make Irish poets' names well known worldwide. I think Austin Clarke is a major poet and a serious chronicler of life in the modern Ireland in all its variety and all its absurdity.

25

JEANANNE CROWLEY

Jeananne Crowley, actress and journalist, was born and raised in Dublin. In the late 1970s she joined the National Theatre in London performing in *Tamburlaine the Great, John Gabriel Borkman* and *The Lady From Maxims*. During the 1980s she lived in London, appearing in many television series, including the award-winning *Tenko* and *Reilly, Ace of Spies*. From London she contributed regularly to *The Irish Times* and as a weekly columnist for the *Sunday Tribune* as well as writing for *The Sunday Times* and *The Guardian*. Back in Dublin she took the title role in *The Real Charlotte* for Granada Television and appeared in the Gate Theatre in such productions as *The Double Dealer* and *Betrayal* by Harold Pinter, and in *After Easter* by Anne Devlin in Belfast. She produced and played the lead in *Spenser's Laye* which she took to the Edinburgh Festival. She has presented *The Sunday Show* for RTE Radio and won an Irish Life Independent Award for her contribution to the arts.

Jeananne Crowley, looking at your bookshelves, the first thing that strikes me is how incredibly well organised you are. You have a section, for example on Ireland and the Irish theatre with a book I see here called 'The Early Irish Stage' by William Smith Clarke which covers the period in Irish theatre from the earliest times to 1720.

Well, first of all, I have to say I'm not really that organised. The fact that part of my bookshelves is organised around Ireland is because I get a lot of visitors over, having lived abroad for so long, and these visitors all want to know about Irish politics and history and literature and the theatre. So I try to keep those books together so that when they come down of a morning and want something to read about Ireland I can point them to these shelves. *The Early Irish Stage* is a particular favourite because I'm a great believer in the continuity of life and we actors are not the first generation who suffered waiting for the agent to call. Nor are we the first who suffered from theatres collapsing around us.

In December 1670, at the height of the play-going season, Smock Alley came to a spectacular halt. On the afternoon of Monday 26th December during a gala holiday performance of Bartholomew Fair, Ben Jonson's biting satire, the theatre galleries suddenly collapsed. The falling weight of timbers and people, according to one eye-witness, hurt a great many and killed one poor girlie, a daughter of Mr Siemen that lived with my mother and three other persons. But, God be praised, the rest had a miraculous escape. The crash happened, according to another spectator, in the third act when the stocks had been brought upon the stage to put the puritans in.

Three hundred years later, in 1970, I found myself on stage in the Olympia Theatre in Dublin one lunchtime when part of the upper circle collapsed onto both the proscenium arch and the orchestra pit.

Staying with the theatre, I see you have the great actress Ellen Terry's 'Correspondence with George Bernard Shaw'.

Do you know, the most interesting thing about that is they never actually met. The things you could do before the telephone! They never met and this fact became quite significant for both of them. Shaw needed *not* to meet Ellen Terry in a peculiar way, yet they had a long love affair by letter. They wrote every day to each other. Every performance she gave he commented on. Every play he wrote he sent her a draft. They were a tremendous spiritual encouragement to each other. I think Shaw is the patron saint of actresses, because he never described them as fallen women; in those days being an actress was not exactly considered socially desirable. Shaw described what he calls the 'socially promiscuous' world of the theatre in a way that is typically his:

> As no extra money is attracted to the pay boxes by the social standing of the performers, talent is everything, pedigree nothing. You can rub shoulders in the theatre with persons of every degree, an order of precedence you must accept in which a person born in a caravan may be estimated and paid more highly than one born in a palace. It takes a revolution

to produce such a state of things outside the theatre; inside the theatre it is ready-made and inevitable.

Here's a book by a remarkable lady, the great nineteenth-century society hostess, Lady Morgan, and you have here her memoirs.

Actually, Lady Morgan is my heroine. If I had to pick one woman in the whole of Irish political philosophy and history it would have to be her. She was the first Irishwoman to make it in Britain and she was one of the first women, Irish or otherwise, to make her living by the fruit of her own literary labours. She did run a salon in Dublin for a while and a popular nineteenth-century ballad had the line 'Daniel O'Connell on his soap box and Lady Morgan making tay'.

Her real name was Sydney Owenson and her father, an actor from Galway called Mac Owen, went off to London and, on the advice of David Garrick, changed his name to Owenson. He was a terrible failure at Covent Garden so he came back to Dublin and started a company at the Smock Alley Theatre and became one of the first of the Irish actor/managers. He never wanted his daughter to become an actress and she wrote in her memoirs: 'I think he is probably right. Being an actress is somewhere between being a duchess and being a whore with the likelihood of experiencing both states at one stage or another.' Indeed, she became an acclaimed writer and a very fashionable writer whose most successful novel was *The Wild Irish Girl*. My theory about Lady Morgan is that her lifetime was her most successful work of fiction. Her novels are melodramatic and unreadable today, but in her life she aroused the most incredibly vituperative criticism. A critic called John Wilson Croker, originally from Dublin, devoted seventeen pages in the *Edinburgh Quarterly* to shredding one of her novels. Byron loved her but Croker hated her and called her 'this audacious worm'. When I perform my one-woman show on Lady Morgan I'll have to call it *That Audacious Worm*.

You have a lot of volumes of poetry on your shelves. The first volume I see is 'Penguin Modern Poets 10 – The Mersey Sound or the Liverpool Poets'.

You know, when you are learning poetry at school you have to learn it for examinations. This was the first-ever poetry book I bought out of my own volition and hundreds of thousands of others bought it as well. This particular edition which features the poems of Adrian Henri, Roger McGough and Brian Patten are the ones which sold thousands of copies. I think it was because lyricism and modern lyrics were becoming popular through pop groups like the Beatles. I love Roger McGough; he was the first and only poet I fell in love with both in real life and in verse.

> Discretion is the better part of Valerie
> though all of her is nice
> lips as warm as strawberries
> eyes as cold as ice
> The very best of everything
> only will suffice
> Not for her potatoes
> and puddings made of rice
>
> Not for her potatoes
> and puddings made of rice
> she takes carbohydrates
> like God takes advice

Here's a poet I don't know – Stephen Vincent Benét. Who is he?

I'm a great lover of narrative verse and I love poetry that rhymes. I love Hilaire Belloc; for instance:

> Matilda told such dreadful lies
> It made one gasp and stretch one's eyes.
> Her Aunt who had from her earliest youth
> Had had a strict regard for truth
> Attempted to believe Matilda
> The effort very nearly killed her.

Stephen Vincent Benét wrote a wonderful poem in the 1920s called 'American Names', and here's one tiny bit of it which I like.

> I have fallen in love with American names
> The sharp names that never get fat.

The snakeskin titles of mining claims
The plumed war bonnet of Medicine Hat
Tucson and Deadwood and Lost Mule Flat.

I shall not rest quiet in Montparnasse
I shall not live easy at Winchelsea
You may bury my body in Sussex Grass
You may bury my tongue at Champ Medi
I shall not be there. I shall rise and pass.
Bury my heart at Wounded Knee.

I'm sure that last line inspired the title of that great study of the American Indians. There are also narrative poets like Banjo Patterson who wrote 'The Ballad of Snowy River'. He was an Irish Aussie, I presume, and as popular over there as Hilaire Belloc ever was here.

Here's a very new-looking volume called 'From the Morning of the World', an anthology of Japanese poetry translated by Graeme Wilson.

This is my most exciting recent find. Everybody should have one. For me it explains and explores the continuity of emotional relationships. The anthology is translated from the Japanese by Graeme Wilson, who lived in Japan for a very long time, and the poems are from the seventh and eighth centuries. To me the Japanese are brilliant at synthesising thought and paring it down. Here we're verbose, talk a lot and use twenty words where one will do. The Japanese are quite the opposite. From the anthology here's one called 'Loneliness':

Darling, when you do not come
My world becomes a blur
Of loneliness so bitter
It would sharpen vinegar.

Yet, if you do come, afterwards
One feels yet lonelier.

Anonymous (late seventh century)

26

EAMON DUNPHY

Eamon Dunphy was born in Drumcondra in Dublin and educated at Sandymount High School. He was a professional footballer with Manchester United and Milwall from 1960 to 1977. There followed a successful career as a journalist with *The Sunday Tribune* and often controversial columnist with the *Sunday Independent*. He is a frequent broadcaster on radio and television on topics as diverse as sport and politics. His publications include *Only A Game?* and *Unforgettable Fire, A Strange Kind of Glory*. He lists as his hobbies conversation, golf, music and reading.

Eamon Dunphy, you live in a house where, I think it would be true to say, books have almost taken over your life.

That's true – they're all over the place and I'm not very well organised. I'm aware of their presence. I'm the kind of person who gives books away and lives to regret it. What I tend to do now is buy a couple of copies of a favourite book. But the memory of the book always stays with you and the pleasure in giving books to friends is immense, so I wouldn't say I'm possessive to the point where I don't do it.

I see two or three books by a friend of yours, Anthony Cronin – 'Dead as Doornails', 'Collected Poems' and 'The Life of Riley'.

These books are special to me. Tony's poems are very distinct and I think he is a great poet. I have a sympathy for the kinds of things he wants to write about. As for *Dead as Doornails*, I'm intensely curious about that period in Irish literary and bohemian life in the '40s and '50s. I would read Patrick Kavanagh a lot and I find the Dublin he depicts in his later poems fascinating and sad in its bitterness and sadness. Myles na Gopaleen and Brendan Behan are also depicted as tragic figures. I think the sadness and isolation in the kind of Dublin that was, in comparison to the access writers today like Brian Friel have to Broadway and the outside world, are very vividly portrayed here. The characters in Cronin's book are trapped here and I think it's a classic of loneliness and frustration. In a certain way I like the bleakness of that time, and I think I would have enjoyed the sad melancholy of being alive at that time.

There's a lot of melancholy tinged with bleakness in the next book I see on your shelves, 'The Collected Poems of Philip Larkin'.

Larkin is a very bleak poet and I can relate to him quite easily. He's a sad, lonely, romantic figure. The real Larkin is rich and there is so much to his poetry that is universal. He is a very English poet in many ways, but in other ways what he is writing about is common to us all. I read Larkin constantly and, like all great poets, you recognise your life in the poetry. There are many lines in Larkin which mean a great deal to me, but there is a poem called 'Aubade' which I think is his greatest poem about the horror of death.

> There is a special way of being afraid
> No trick dispels. Religion used to try,
> The vast moth-eaten musical brocade
> Created to pretend we never die.
> And specious stuff that says *No rational being*
> *Can fear a thing it will not feel*, not seeing
> That this is what we fear – no sight, no sound,
> No touch or taste or smell, nothing to think with,
> Nothing to love or link with,
> The anaesthetic from which none come round.

You're a great reader of biographies, and I see Richard Ellmann's classic biography of James Joyce on your shelves.

Joyce was an heroic figure, probably the most heroic Irishman of this century. I like the Ellmann biography because it is incredibly comprehensive. I know it has been criticised, but I think it is a work of amazing scholarship. Joyce is a hero, and the fascination of a book like that is to imagine the life and the loneliness and the struggle.

Books on American politics seems to figure largely on your shelves. I'm looking at a couple of biographies of Lyndon B. Johnson, 'Means of Ascent' and 'The Path of Power' by Robert Caro.

P. J. Mara gave me a present of those to show me how pristine Fianna Fáil was and what the nature of politics really is. Johnson was an extraordinary character. These books go up only to 1941 when he was still in the Senate, a long time before he became a national figure as President of the United States. The corruption and wheeler-dealing in Texan politics, and Johnson's own personal character, his behaviour towards his wife and his incredible single-minded pursuit of power, all show him to be a very insecure and deeply flawed man. He had a gargantuan appetite for power and he consumed people. These books made some of our contemporary Irish political villains seem quite harmless.

Staying in America, I see a biography of sorts of the writer Norman Mailer by Peter Manso: 'Norman Mailer – His Life and Times'.

Manso is a friend of Mailer who hangs out with the New York literary crowd. He calls it an oral biography where he goes around and interviews everybody that Mailer ever knew, including Mailer and his seven wives and all the people he fought with and loved. It's a tour around literary New York and a gossipy insight into Mailer's personal and working life. It's a fascinating book in a light sort of way. It's not a literary biography, but it's a way of writing about a subject if you have that access to a figure like Norman Mailer.

Another exponent of the new journalism in the United States is Tom Wolfe.

When I began as a journalist I was very influenced by Tom Wolfe. I read all his essays and I've read everything he ever wrote, including the late fiction. He was a seminal figure for journalists. He and Mailer created the new journalism where the writer makes himself the central figure in the story and becomes subjective. I was in my thirties when I began in journalism, and I had to learn what I was getting into. I learned a great deal from both Mailer and Wolfe.

You greatly admire the Irish writer, Colm Toibin, and I see you have his travel book 'Homage to Barcelona' side by side with his novel 'The South'.

The South is a brilliant, beautiful novel and *Homage to Barcelona* is much more than a travel book, brilliantly written as is everything Colm Toibin writes. His prose glows with humour and has a distinct feel to it. He is probably our finest young writer's, and his book *Walking Along the Border* is a book unlike anything else written about Northern Ireland.

As a journalist and biographer who is concerned with style, it's not surprising that you have George Orwell's 'Inside the Whale and Other Essays' on your shelves.

Orwell I've read going back to the time I was playing football. Orwell has been a huge influence on me and on my generation. He doesn't write stylishly but he writes very plainly. There is so much substance, so much wisdom and so much courage in his writing. When you read his essays you realise he had so much courage to go against the grain of his time. He was a very independent-minded and singular man. I read his essays frequently and I often draw inspiration from his writings. I find I can return to the essays and discover something new every time.

Everybody would expect you to have a lot of books about sport on your shelves, but I don't see many here.

There are not many because not much that is very good has been written about sport. Sport has not inspired good writing in these islands, although in America it has. Sadly, the sports writing we have in these islands is pretty poor and I don't read it for pleasure at all. When you read a book you want to get into another world, another life, escape from the mundane.

27

DAVID NORRIS

David Norris is a Senator representing Trinity College and a retired university lecturer. He is a renowned Joycean scholar and a tireless fighter for human rights, best known for his action in the Irish courts and subsequently in the Court of Human Rights to have the Irish laws on homosexuality changed. He has also been a vociferous spokesman for the preservation of Georgian Dublin and is a member of the AIDS Foundation. He is Irish Trustee of the International James Joyce Foundation, and Chairman of the James Joyce Cultural Centre in Dublin. His publications include countless articles and contributions in journals and books on a wide range of subjects from literary to sociological and cultural heritage. He is a witty and gifted raconteur who has toured widely his one-man show on Joyce. He is a frequent lecturer on the international circuit and a regular radio and television broadcaster at home.

David Norris, here in your elegantly restored Georgian house in North Great Georges Street, we're surrounded by books. I'm not at all surprised that the first volume I see on your shelves is the recent biography of Oscar Wilde by Richard Ellmann. A great biography?

Well, a very good biography but not I think in the same class as his biography of James Joyce, which is his most famous book. I knew Dick Ellmann over twenty years and I realised that towards the end of the period he was writing the biography of Oscar Wilde he was seriously ill with motor neuron disease and I think that shows in the work. There isn't the same energy, vitality and commitment. Also, in a sense, when he was writing about Joyce, Ellmann was extolling his own virtues: he was a good family man, a man of modesty, a man who was not a snob and didn't use his great intelligence and brilliance as a scholar to intimidate. He knew and could empathise with Joyce. He knew the contents of Joyce's pockets on any given day. In fact, he was an encyclopedist of Joyce. With the Oscar Wilde biography there is an intelligent understanding of Wilde from the

outside. I got the feeling that, sympathetic though he was to the whole gay issue, Ellmann did not fully understand its complexity. There are elements of the stereotype in his portrait of Wilde. For example, Ellmann talks about Saint Sebastian being an icon for all gay men. I only heard of Saint Sebastian in the last couple of years, so he certainly wasn't an icon of mine. In the same way he missed out on things in the Wilde biography, whereas in the Joyce book he made the connections in every detail.

Moving on from Oscar Wilde, I see you have a book here called 'Becoming a Man – Half a Life Story' by Paul Monette. Who is he and why is this autobiography called 'Half a Life Story'?

Well, in a sense it relates to Oscar Wilde because Wilde found it so difficult to realise himself as a gay man. Paul Monette was a young American writer who denied his sexuality for a long time. He was a teacher of English in the American equivalent of our secondary school while he was making a reputation as a writer of fiction. Gradually he came to realise himself and to develop a long-term relationship with a lover who died of AIDS. He was forced by circumstances to face his own sexuality, to understand it and to appreciate it. That's why his autobiography is called *Becoming a Man*. It's an extraordinary, moving, honest and realistic book, and the kind of book I think I would recommend to anyone who wasn't gay to help them understand the experience.

We have to talk about James Joyce, and you have a huge Joycean library which has grown alarmingly over the past twenty or thirty years. You've chosen an edition of 'Finnegans Wake'.

My collection of books by and about Joyce I am giving to the James Joyce Centre in 35 North Great Georges Street. One of the most beautiful things in *Finnegans Wake* is a description of the River Liffey which is not hackneyed as some of the other parts of the book have now become by repetition. The key to *Finnegans Wake* is to listen to the sounds. This is the sound of the River Liffey as it comes tumbling down the foothills of the Dublin mountains out towards the bay.

With a beck, with a spring, all her rillringlets shaking, rocks drops in her tachie, tramtokens in her hair, all waived to a point and then all inuendation, little old-fashioned mummy, little wonderful mummy, ducking under bridges, bellhopping the weirs, dodging by a bit of bog, rapid-shooting round the bends, by Tallaght's green hills and the pools of the phooka and a place they call it Blessington and slipping sly by Sallynoggin, as happy as the day is wet, babbling, bubbling, chattering to herself, deloothering the fields on their elbows leaning with the sloothering slide of her, giddy-gaddy, grannyma, gossipaceous Anna Livia.

He lifts the lifewand and the dumb speak.

- Quoiquoiquoiquoiquoiquoiquoi!

That little detail at the end is the wonderful *Book of Kells*-like detail, in the way in which the medieval monks in the illuminated manuscripts used to put in, for example, a cat chasing a mouse among the tendrils of the manuscript's illustrations. That's a duck quacking as it is borne down along by the River Liffey towards the city of Dublin, and it's a very educated duck because it's been educated at Belvedere or Loreto College and it's talking French, saying 'quoi-quoi-quoi-quoi?' Like a lot of other people the two poor little ducks are puzzled about what is going on in this extraordinary book.

I think *Finnegans Wake* is like a play which only exists when it is being acted out aloud. To me *Finnegans Wake* exists only when it is being read. I think Joyce was actively involved in something here, like a kind of Frankenstein. The inert elements of Joyce's consciousness are retained here in the book, and that multi-faceted consciousness comes to life once more, is revived and defies death, when someone performs or reads *Finnegans Wake*. It's a kind of magical ritual.

Moving into the '90s the next book I see here is Irish actor Gabriel Byrne's memoir 'Pictures in My Head', published last year.

It's one of the most beautifully written books I've read in a very long time. It's essentially a series of autobiographical fragments with a clean, sharp style. The eye for detail, the sense of character and the complete honesty are almost Joycean. I've bought several copies of this remarkable book and sent one to a friend in Hollywood who is trying to become an actor; I thought it would help him to keep his feet on the ground. I also gave a copy of this book to James Joyce's nephew, Ken Monaghan, and he said it was one of the most moving and delightful books he had read.

The next book I see was was a great popular bestseller of recent years: 'Wild Swans – Three Daughters of China' by Jung Chang.

I didn't read it until after my first visit to China because I'm a sort of inverted snob who, when people say I must read a particular popular fashionable book, says yes and I'll buy it but I won't read it. After my first visit to China I read this book and found it very haunting, in particular the figure of Jung Chang's father who was a most honourable, decent man. He had the ideal of communism and desperately tried to live it out, even at the expense and disadvantage of his own children. Even he, at the end of the day, was forced to see that the regime was manipulative, corrupt and had let him down, and that Mao Tse Tung was just a sort of overgrown balloon hanging over Tiananmen Square. I read this book with particular pleasure because I was in China recently visiting two old friends who have translated Joyce's *Ulysses* into Mandarin. The two translators, having been so badly treated during the Cultural Revolution, have now become heroes in China and the first edition of their translation of *Ulysses* has been sold out.

I see a novel on your shelves with an intriguing title. It's called 'Fried Green Tomatoes at the Whistle Stop Café' by a writer called Fannie Flagg.

This is a marvellous story and I can thank RTE for my discovering this book because it turned up as a lat-night film on television. It's a story of a young woman who has a miserable marriage until she meets this old dear in a retirement home and they begin this wonderful relationship. The old girl had a restaurant called The Whistle Stop Café and her great recipe was for fried green tomatoes and all the locals come in and you get this marvellous gallery of characters. It's beautifully, freshly written, comic and celebratory of life, and celebratory of the fact that the old people can actually live life fully to the end and this old bird does. It's a heart-warming marvellous story.

You've made a particular study of the Irish short story, and I see you have many volumes by Irish writers. What is it that attracts you to the Irish short story?

It's the vigour and the insight and the understanding of the figure of the outsider. In particular, I was lucky enough to have been taught at Trinity College by Frank O'Connor, who was one of the great short-story writers. One of my favourite stories of his is called 'The Drunkard' which is about the father who is always going on the batter. He has a few months of sobriety but a funeral is coming up and the mother sends the young son along with him to act as a brake. Eventually of course they go into a pub, the father orders a pint of stout, turns his back on it with an air of a great luxury because he knows there's six months of abstinence behind him and an eternity of pleasure in front of him. The child pulls at his coat but the father ignores him.

> I was still thirsty. I found if I stood on tiptoe I could just reach Father's glass, and the idea occurred to me that it would be interesting to know what the contents were like. He had his back to it and wouldn't notice. I took down the glass and sipped cautiously. It was a terrible disappointment. I was astonished that he could even drink such stuff. It looked as if he had never tried lemonade.
>
> I should have advised him about lemonade but he was holding forth himself in a great style. I heard him say that bands were a great addition to a funeral. He put his arms in the position of someone holding a rifle in reverse and hummed a few bars of Chopin's Funeral March. Crowley

nodded reverently. I took a longer drink and began to see that porter might have its advantages. I felt pleasantly elevated and philosophic. Father hummed a few bars of the Dead March in Saul. It was a nice pub and a very fine funeral, and I felt sure that poor Mr Dooley in Heaven must be highly gratified. At the same time I thought they might have given him a band. As Father said, bands were a great addition.

But the wonderful thing about porter was the way it made you stand aside, or rather float aloft like a cherub rolling on a cloud, and watch yourself with your legs crossed, leaning against a bar counter, not worrying about trifles but thinking deep, serious, grown-up thoughts about life and death. Looking at yourself like that, you couldn't helping thinking after a while how funny you looked, and suddenly you got embarrassed and wanted to giggle. By the time I had finished the pint, that phase too had passed; I found it hard to put back the glass, the counter seemed to have grown so high. Melancholia was supervening again.

You have there the wonderful parody of adult drunkenness in the mind of the child. I admire, too, absolutely one of the great unsung artists of the short story, Mary Lavin. She has such an insight into the life of small town and manages to universalise them so that parochial things become really universal. She has an insight into the human heart and she writes with such an intuitive understanding of the human spirit.

28

LELIA DOOLAN

Lelia Doolan is currently Chairperson of the Irish Film Board and Director of the Galway Film Fleadh. She has in turn been a television and theatre director, an actress, journalist and lecturer. She was formerly Head of Light Entertainment in RTE Television and won a Jacobs Award for her direction of *The Plough and the Stars*. From 1971 to 1973 she was Artistic Director of the Abbey Theatre. In RTE Television she was producer/director of *The Riordans* and she founded *Seven Days*, the flagship current-affairs programme. She has had roles in various documentary and film activities, including executive producer on *Clash of the Ash* for television and producer of the film *Reefer and the Model*.

Lelia Doolan, film producer, lecturer, author and perpetual student, the books I see here on your shelves reflect some of the many and varied interests you have pursued in your life. I'm looking at 'The Fortunes of the Irish Language' by Daniel Corkery in a two-shilling red-covered edition, 'Imeachtaí na Teanga Gaeilge'. You've a strong interest in the Irish language.

I suppose I'm a kind of book kleptomaniac, and when you look through someone's bookshelves it's a kind of personal archaeology, in a way. You go back to things you began with – all the novels you bought, every Penguin edition you could find of a particular writer. I remember going through all the novels of Patrick White and everything Muriel Spark wrote and Iris Murdoch too. Then things begin to change and you read other books. This particular study of the Irish language by Daniel Corkery was given me by my sister, Mary. I believe this very passionate book would rouse somebody who was stone dead with its feel for the Irish language, the history of the language and all of it intertwined with the history of the country. There was a famous altercation between Daniel Corkery and that great scholar Monsignor Pádraig de Brún, based on the question as to what was the best way to revive the Irish language. Corkery, apparently was very keen on the native writers as the source of the revival, while de Brún was very much a European and an internationalist. I feel that it was a tragedy that the two were not able to agree and come together. Also, at that time I read *The Aran Islands* by John Millington Synge and I have a lovely recent edition from the Blackstaff Press with drawings by Jack Yeats. It's an absolutely lovely book, a joy to feel, to touch and to hold.

Here's a book that reflects your lifelong interest in the theatre. It's 'Put Money in Thy Purse' by Michael Mac Liammor, the diary of the filming of Orson Welles' 'Othello'.

There have been wonderful books written on the making of films but this is a truly great book. There's a piece at the very beginning where Michael is in bed after a nervous breakdown following flu', where he thinks he was possessed by evil spirits. A telegram arrives from Orson Welles.

> Dearest Michael – enthusiastically repeat offer made by me to Hilton – you play Iago with me in Othello film. Stop. Can you come to Paris to arrange things? Stop. When can you come? Stop. I will try to come to Dublin if you can't come to Paris. Stop. Love to you both. Orson.

That's the sort of mood in which the whole thing began and it steadily got worse. They ran out of money, things went wrong, people got sick and Orson had to leave the film to go and raise money. Rita Hayworth crops up. In one section Michael talks about Welles, the director, and the terrifying yet exhilarating experience of filming *Othello*.

> I never again will have anything but the deepest respect for any actor who can move or speak at all, however ignobly, before a camera. Having taken what seems the only possible course – blind unquestioning obedience to, and dependence on, the will of the director. This is easy to do before the day's work begins by the abandoning of my face at six each morning to Santoli and Vasca who paint, beard and bewig me as I sit inert in a chair, not even glancing into a mirror, a towel tied under my chin to keep me, I suppose, from

dribbling on my doublet. This over, I totter on to the set, will soon have to be led, probably carried and wait, generally for several hours, to be told what to do. The result of this is a form of complete and paralytic inanity. For the past two days I have had to be instructed on how to raise my arm, turn my head or place my feet and have little doubt that if this continues I shall soon be led away like Oswald in *Ghosts* babbling, 'The sun, Orson! Give me the sun!'.

It's a wonderful book and beautifully written.

Here's a Penguin Classic you bought for six shillings – Dostoevsky's 'The Brothers Karamazov'. You bought it secondhand and it looks well thumbed and well read.

I read and re-read *The Brothers Karamozov*. I think the whole universe is somehow encapsulated in Dostoevsky's work, all of the dread moments, all of the hilarious moments, all of the tragic moments, all of the big moments and questions like 'Who is it then that is laughing at us? Is God the one who is laughing at us?' It brings me to another book which I think is the best account of life in the Stalinist purges and life in the prison camps. It's called *Journey into the Whirlwind* and the second part is *Within the Whirlwind,* and they are written by Eugenia Ginsberg. She was a teacher in Tartar Russia who, with her husband, was taken away after the murder of Kirov when the purges began. It is not just a book of tremendous humanity and endurance, it is also a book of great humour and poetry. There is one episode she recalls when they were all incarcerated in a train travelling across to Siberia where they eventually were sent to prison camps. The train guards had warned them about no reading, no talking, no books, but one of the prisoners began reciting a great poem by Pushkin. The guards said, 'No books allowed,' and they stopped the train and opened the carriage. There was no book. This woman simply knew the poem by heart and could say it from beginning to end. At the end of one of the chapters, when they are still on the train, the author learns that she has been sentenced to ten years 'actual penal servitude and five years' loss of liberty. After they had been actually sentenced she writes,

I wasn't crying but my heart was pounding with excitement. I wanted her to go on and on calling me comrade. To think that such a word still existed and that someone could use it to me. So I was not just Cell Number 3, North Side, after all. The train was bound eastwards towards the camps. Penal servitude – what bliss!

Eugenia Ginsberg saw through it in the end, but it was an amazing life to survive.

I see the first novel written by Belfast-born Glen Patterson – it's called 'Burning Your Own' and it's quite a powerful novel.

I lived in Belfast for some years in the '70s and this is a wonderfully powerful book of childhood observations and not just about one side of the political and religious divide. It's about a young boy, Mal Martin, and his family and the whole boredom of home and the domestic life are conveyed wonderfully. You also get the absolute dream-like fantasies of a character who lives in a sort of subterranean world, nearly. The novel is just an absolute *tour de force*.

Staying with the North of Ireland, I see you have Father Des Wilson's 'An End to Silence'.

This was published in 1985 and Des Wilson is an extraordinary man who has lived within the maelstrom of Northern Ireland for so many years now. This is a very intelligent book which wasn't appreciated properly when it came out. Wilson is trying to analyse the different aspects of the parties to the Northern situation, and he is pointing out the role of the Church, the role of the British government, the military – clerical axis and the possibilities for democracy. He is pointing out that without the possibility for all parties to have a voice there isn't going to be any solution there. Simply describing people as thugs and terrorists and criminals is just delaying the process of peace.

Here's an interesting-looking paperback. The cover shows an African hut with a straw roof from which sprouts a complicated array of television aerials. The book is called 'Oh What a Blow that Phantom Gave Me', by Edmund Carpenter.

Edmund Carpenter is an anthropologist and that is one of the subjects I studied in Belfast. This is a book about the media. Carpenter was a consultant who went down to Papua New Guinea to bring the natives some notion of the modern media, and he discovered, of course, that they had better knowledge about this than the experts. The title is a phrase from one of my favourite books, *Don Quixote* by Cervantes, and this book by Carpenter opens your eyes to the way the media has permeated the Third World and how they [the people of the Third World] have come to terms with that aspect of First World civilisation.

29

JOE O'CONNOR

Joe O'Connor was born in Dublin in 1963. His first novel, *Cowboys and Indians*, was shortlisted for the Whitbread Prize, and his first collection of short stories, *True Believers*, was widely acclaimed. Since then his second novel, *Desperadoes*, has been published, along with a collection of his journalism and occasional writings. He has also written film and television scripts and a biography of the Irish poet Charles Donnelly, *Even the Olives Are Bleeding*. His first stage play, *Red Roses and Petrol*, was presented in Dublin and London by Pigsback Theatre Company. He is a regular columnist with *The Sunday Tribune* and in 1993 won the Macaulay Fellowship of the Irish Arts Council.

Joe O'Connor, the first book I see here on your shelves is a relatively recent novel by an Irish writer, and it's called 'The Fabulists' by Philip Casey.

I first came across Philip Casey as a poet and always admired his work. This is his first novel, published by Lilliput Press in Dublin 1994. I approached it with some trepidation since it was a first novel, but I found it amazingly accomplished. It's a book I've read now three or four times, and it has that really magnificent quality that great novels have, where you find yourself thinking about them a few weeks after you finish reading them. You are walking down the street and the characters in the novel are so vivid that you almost find yourself saying, if you see something in the street, 'I wonder what would that guy in the novel think about that?' It's a love story set in contemporary Dublin and that's a difficult thing to do because Dublin novelists sometimes tend to characterise Dublin as a gas place full of incredibly funny taxi drivers and bawdy nights in pubs and all the rest. But the Dublin that Philip Casey conjures up reminds me of Dermot Bolger's Dublin in a way, it's just so real and absolutely recognisable right from the first page. It's a very tender love story. What holds the affair together is the fact that these two people meet once a week and they tell each other stories. So as well as the

story in the novel working very well on its own merits, it also builds into a metaphor for the power of stories generally. I found that aspect of the novel very moving. It's a magnificent book and it's just come out in England and I'm sure it will do very well there for Philip Casey.

Another contemporary Irish novel which features on your shelves is 'A Goat's Song' by Dermot Healy.

This novel is set in the west of Ireland primarily, although it moves around the country quite a lot and part of it is set in Belfast. Dermot Healy and myself are published by the same publishers and we ended up on a reading tour of England and Ireland together which was very wild and very exciting. Dermot is great company and he is full of life and humour. This novel is so dark and is also a kind of doomed love story. I don't know why I like all these doomed love stories – maybe it says something about me! It's such a vivid novel, and it has an odd thing that some of the work of Yeats has, where very specific details or very specific lives take on the resonance of a whole society. In some way this book, which is really about two people, one Catholic and one Protestant, manages to be about the whole of this island without being boring or lecturing in any way or without being a work of propaganda. It skirts being clichéd from time to time. Some of the characters, if you read the book in a shallow way, might even seem to be clichés, but Healy takes these clichés and he completely inverts them. Again, it has the same quality as the Philip Casey novel – it's just totally memorable. It's very funny in places but basically extremely tragic.

Flannery O'Connor is an American writer you admire and I see you have 'Mystery and Manners – Occasional Prose', selected and edited by Sally and Robert Fitzgerald.

I've always loved her short stories. It's quite interesting about Flannery O'Connor's work, in that she was a very devout Catholic, which comes across in her work again and again. She is one of the few people who can write about religious subjects in an absolutely direct way but in a very inclusive way, even if you don't share the ideology – which I absolutely don't. The passion with which she writes is very affecting and quite seductive. She's such a skilful writer and her sentences are so seductive that when I saw this book, which contains essays about her own writing, I was interested in seeing what her own reflections might be and some of her words of advice. I'm always interested in hearing what really great writers have to say about writing and the book is full of wonderful things like the following in an essay called 'The Nature and Aim of Fiction'.

> One of the most common spectacles is that of a person of really fine sensibility trying to write fiction by using this quality alone. This type of writer will put down one intensely emotional or keenly perceptive sentence after the other and the result will be complete dullness. The fact is that the materials of the fiction writer are the humblest. Fiction is about everything human and we are made out of dust and if you scorn getting yourself dusty then you shouldn't try to write fiction. It's not a grand enough job for you.

There's a marvellous truth to that. I love Flannery O'Connor's fiction but her instructions on writing are marvellous as well.

An American novelist who has come very much into prominence over the past few years is Cormac McCarthy and you have his novel 'The Crossing' here on your shelves.

Cormac McCarthy has gone from being a cult figure in the States to being a universally recognised fine writer on this side of the Atlantic, more so in Britain and Ireland than in America, where he sells very well but lives as a bit of a recluse. He is well known for never appearing in public and he has won all these huge literary awards which he has never bothered turning up to collect. He lives in a little shack in El Paso in Texas where he has been writing for thirty years. The novels are very dark but brilliant evocations of the American landscape in particular. Any novelist knows what a difficult thing it is to be able to write about a place in any new way. When you look at a mountain or a lake you often feel the descriptions of it all have been done before, but McCarthy has a strange cinematic quality to the work. You read a page of it and you could be absolutely there – you don't even have to close your eyes. The way he writes about landscape, nature and animals too is really eerie. This book is about a boy who captures a wolf in America and he brings the wolf back to Mexico. The characterisation of the wolf is almost as complex as the characterisation of the boy. He is almost a magician of language, although it is not a style that I would try to emulate myself. I think reading a few pages of Cormac McCarthy is like getting in a nice warm bath where you just luxuriate in the skill and the facility he has for language.

I know that Derek Mahon is one of your favourite poets and I see his 'Selected Poems' here on your shelves.

I love Derek Mahon's work. What I love about it is that he is so skilled, he is almost like a classical writer in ways. He tends to use fairly strict metres and rhythms and what might be called academic rhyming schemes. You can actually study how his poems work and how they are put together. To me the current vogue in poetry for putting down on the page just what you feel isn't particularly interesting. Paul Durcan, for example, is a magnificent writer and his poem have that appearance, but I think the current phase of Durcan imitators could learn a lot from a poet as skilled as Mahon. There's one short poem of his which is a good illustration of what I've been saying.

Nostalgias

The chair squeaks in a high wind,
Rain falls from its branches;
The kettle yearns for the mountain,
The soap for the sea.
In a tiny stone church
On a desolate headland
A lost tribe is singing 'Abide With Me'.

The language Mahon uses is so pressurised with meaning it is absolutely charged and a poem like that, which is only seven lines, just says so much. I find his work a real pleasure.

You talked earlier about younger Irish writers Philip Casey and Dermot Healy, but I see you have a work by an Irish writer of an older generation – 'Christ in the Fields' by Eugene McCabe.

I wasn't aware of this book until this summer, when I spent some time in Annaghmakerrig in County Monaghan in this house owned by the Arts Council where writers can go for a while and work. One of the great pleasures of Annaghmakerrig is that there are so many books there that you can invariably pick up something you haven't heard about and start to read. This book consists of three long short stories set around the Border region and in the North of Ireland. McCabe's great tragic subject is the sectarianism of Ireland, and in some ways this book is just a re-statement of that. There was a lot on the news at the time about the peace process and the talks that were going on, and I couldn't help feeling that every single politician who was involved in sprouting platitudes about peace in Ireland should be forced to read Eugene McCabe's *Christ in the Fields*. It would give them some idea of just how deep this problem is, but out of it McCabe manages to make a very beautiful work. It's almost like an act of mourning for that society, and is extremely powerful.

I know you are a great fan of Flann O'Brien/Brian O'Nolan/Myles na Gopaleen and I see you have a well-battered paperback edition of 'At Swim-Two-Birds'.

I could have quite easily spoken to you for the whole time just about Flann O'Brien. *At Swim-Two-Birds* is probably the funniest novel I've ever read. This particular copy is of some sentimental value because my first girlfriend gave it to me when I was sixteen. It was the first serious novel I read that wasn't on the school course and since that time I've moved a lot but somehow or other this book always survives following me around. Flann O'Brien is still the great unsung hero in that I don't think he has ever got the international reputation he deserves. He was an extremely complex man, full of doubt and fear and self-loathing. In *The Best of Myles*, culled from his columns in *The Irish Times*, he was capable of being incredibly funny and incredibly intelligent as well.

As a practitioner who values prose style I'm not at all surprised to see on your shelves John McGahern's 'Collected Stories'.

I love McGahern and I'm a big fan, but I came to the novels first. This *Collected Stories* is similar to Flannery O'Connor's in that the precision of the language is so striking. He is the great artist of the small moment. In a lot of these stories it appears as if nothing is happening, but in fact huge things are happening underneath the surface. Not much happens in the plot but his really astute perceptions of small moments in people's lives is exquisitely done. It's a great book and one I'm going to come back to again and again for a long time.

30

PAUL FUNGE

Paul Funge, painter, stage designer, musician and teacher, is a native of Gorey, County Wexford and was educated in Newbridge College and St Peter's College, Wexford. He attended the National College of Art in Dublin and while a student there was awarded an Italian government scholarship to study in Florence. He has exhibited his paintings widely to great acclaim in Ireland, Europe, USA, and South America. He was one of the founders of the arts centre concept in Ireland, being one of the first directors of the Project Arts Centre in Dublin and founder of the Arts Centre and Festival in Gorey, County Wexford. In 1978 he was appointed Ireland's first Regional Arts Officer in the Mid-West Region. He has designed sets for the major theatres in Dublin. He is currently the Department of Education's Inspector of Art. His highly distinctive painting has been described as figurative or contemporary figurative, and his portraits of government ministers, writers, academics and pop stars have been highly acclaimed.

Paul Funge, you have had a lifelong love relationship with Spain. You have worked and painted there and you visit Spain every year. I'm not surprised to see a lot of books about Spain on your shelves. I see here a whole section by the Spanish poet Lorca – books by and about Lorca. What is your fascination with Frederico Garcia Lorca?

I suppose the fascination with Spain goes back to my childhood when I had an uncle who studied in Salamanca but he had to leave Spain in the middle of the Spanish Civil War. They all had to abandon their studies and were evacuated back to Ireland. He was left with a network of friends in Spain, many of whom asked him to organise either their offspring to come to be educated in Ireland. I got parachuted in to teach English to a family in Santander way back in 1961 without one word of Spanish. Very shortly after I spent a few summers in the northern Spain. I arrived down in a little village south of Cordoba, very much an Andalusian village. That's where the mystery of Andalusia and Lorca and the poetry began for me. I have a volume of translations of Lorca by Stephen Spender, an extraordinary courageous volume to have brought out in 1939 so soon after Lorca's controversial murder in 1936. I suddenly arrived in sunswept Andalusia to come across a very beautiful poem called 'Romance Sonambulo'.

> Verde que te quiero verde.
> Verde viento. Verdes ramas.
> El barco sobre la mar
> y el cabrollo en la montana.
>
> *Green, how I love you green.*
> *Green wind. Green branches.*
> *The ship upon the sea*
> *And the house in the mountain.*

Well, that's a fairly pedestrian translation by Spender which is quite literal but misses out on the metaphorical magic. Lorca worked in metaphors and an Andalusian based on the gypsy mystique and the gypsy tradition, which had all kinds of very specific metaphoric meanings for colour and for horses and for symbols. For my money Ian Gibson's two-volume biography of Lorca is the best there is. I actually met Ian Gibson in Spain and I find his Lorca biography compelling. He has done a stunning job. Quite apart from his enormous scholarship about the body of Lorca's work, there is a tremendous human interest in the subject. He never loses sight of Lorca the man or of the heroic life and horrendous death of the poet.

You are a great admirer of the Irish poet Seán Ó Riordáin and I see on your shelves his volumes 'Eireaball Spideoige', 'Brosna' and 'Línte Liombo'. In fact you did some illustrations for some of Ó Riordáin's work.

Actually I was very fortunate in having as a friend another eminent Irish writer who was a national schoolteacher, Diarmuid Ó Súilleabháin, who taught me in Gorey, all of whose work I illustrated for Sairséal agus Dill. I had a very happy relationship with that publishing house and was fortunate enough to be asked to illustrate the work of many of their star writers. Seán Ó Riordáin wrote a few lines in *Línte Liombo* in response to my modest illustrations.

Cá bhfios dom nárbh iadsan
Dob fhearr a dhéanfadh cúis,
Dob fhearr a chuirfeadh mise
Ins an rud a bhí le ra?
Ach ambasadóirí eile
A sheolas uaim chun siúil
Fé mar ná beadh ina malairt
Ach aicme gan aird.

He is saying there that the illustrations are other means of understanding his poems from another source, another discipline. Poetry is one way of distilling the essences of life, whereas visual imagery is another method of encapsulating the nugget of essence or existence.

You look at a book in very much the same way as you read a work of art.

For me, books that don't transform themselves into a kind of experience that has a similarity to the way you see a painting aren't exciting. We all read light reading, of course, but for me books that grab my attention are books that seem to suspend the beginning, middle and end that exist as a kind of essence of conventional fiction.

You have here a book whose very title has always intrigued me – it's Elizabeth Smart's 'By Grand Central Station I Sat Down and Wept'. What is the attraction of that book for you?

I borrowed that book many years ago from Gary Lombard when I was going through my existentialist period. I empathised so profoundly with that book I have forgotten to give it back to him. Talking of the existentialist, I did go thought a phase of reading Sartre and Genet and Gide. My teacher Diarmuid Ó Súilleabháin, who was a great European, introduced me to many of the great French existentialists. This particular volume here, *The Counterfeiters* by Andre Gide, and Jean Genet's *Our Lady of the Flowers* are both books whose writing plucks the contemporary zing of what it means to live in these complex times.

You have in your time designed for the theatre, and you have here a script of Eduardo Manet's play 'The Nuns'. That was a production you particularly enjoyed designing.

It went on, in fact in the Focus Theatre in Dublin. Tom Hickey and Deirdre O'Connell were stars in it – it was a terrific production. It is still talked of in the folklore of the Focus and the set was virtually impossible to design for such a tiny stage. That set is also talked about in the lore of set design.

I see you have Nobel Prize-winner Elios Canetti's novel 'Audo-da-fe' here on your shelves, a novel Iris Murdoch described as one of the great books of the twentieth century.

That was a book I stumbled upon when I had barely started my annual Spanish visitations. Around the early 1970s I realised he was of Spanish origin. It makes for gripping reading, unusually slanted in how the experience is described. It's like a Cubist picture, in retrospect.

Do you read contemporary Irish fiction?

I read Colm Toibin and Philip Casey, both of whom started their literary careers at the Gorey Arts Festival which I had the dubious distinction of founding. That brought me into contact with some extraordinary writers like American poet John Ashbery, who is now regarded as one of the most important poets of the American surrealist school. Another very important American visitor to Gorey was William Dickey, who is a magnificent poet and I painted his portrait in the Ormond Hotel – the old Ormond before it was done up – in his dingy little bedroom. That portrait is now hanging in the Institute of Art in San Francisco. Yes, indeed, those distant days of the Gorey Arts Festival introduced me to a lot of writers and artists, many of whom became my friends, and opened my eyes to new ways of thinking and reading and new ways of seeing.

31

MICHAEL D. HIGGINS

Michael D. Higgins, was born in Limerick and reared in Newmarket-on-Fergus, County Clare. He was educated at University College, Galway, Indiana University and Manchester University. He has lectured in Political Science and Sociology at University College, Galway and in 1992 won the Sean MacBride International Peace Medal for his work for human rights. He is a Labour TD for Galway West, has twice been Mayor of Galway and is currently Minister for Arts, Culture and the Gaeltacht. He has published two collections of poems, *The Betrayal* (1990) and *The Season of Fire* (1993), both illustrated by Mick Mulcahy. He has written on a wide variety of social, political and cultural issues, and is a frequent broadcaster on radio and television.

Michael D. Higgins, looking at your bookshelves I see that a lot of your books arise out of your interest in politics, sociology and economics.

Interestingly I have done a contradictory thing lately: I have put the literary works to live in a separate place on a separate set of shelves to the ones I regard as practical and short term. There is a kind of golden section in between where you have books that shade into each other and represent my favourite place. These are the ones I tend to return to, an intersection of what you might call poetry, philosophy, literature and history. These are books with a broadly humanistic thrust.

One of the volumes I see which looks well read is 'The House of Gold' by Liam O'Flaherty.

I have come back many times to this book and I have written about it in an essay on the sociology of literature, comparing Liam O'Flaherty with Peadar O'Donnell and others. I raised the question as to how both writers fitted into a realist tradition or not. This book by O'Flaherty was massively controversial in its day, banned from circulation in the British

Empire because of the closeness of the tale itself to the life of a very prominent Galway commercial family. I have used the book, not ransacked it, but used it for a very definite purpose, which is to regard literature not as evidence used by sociologists, but as literary insights that illuminate aspects of reality you would otherwise miss. For example, my interest in the formal sociology of migration misses, because of its concentration of why people leave and how they adjust, the part in the middle, which is transience. Yet this experience of suitcase life is in Patrick McGill and Peadar O'Donnell. The emergence of greed and the underbelly of native capitalism is in *The House of Gold* and it is traced beautifully. This is not to reduce the novel as a story, which is very powerful.

You read a lot of poetry and I see that Patrick Kavanagh's 'Collected Poems' have pride of place here on your shelves.

I've enjoyed Kavanagh very much for a long time. My favourite Kavanagh poem was 'Pegasus' and I used to like to read his early poems written in Dublin, his optimistic period after escaping from Monaghan, and the poems about his room which was a kind of light to the sky through which he saw everything. His later poems are much more depressing. I've been back to Kavanagh recently, because of the things I've been writing, and seeing a deeper significance in my re-reading Kavanagh at fifty years. After his 'Song at Fifty' he has a beautiful poem, 'The Hospital'.

> A year ago I fell in love with the functional ward
> Of a chest hospital: square cubicles in a row
> Plain concrete, wash basins – an art lover's woe.

Poems like that which are celebrations of the miraculous and the ordinary are very powerful to me now. I see a resonance in these poems for myself, and I take great pleasure and see a spiritual celebration in them.

Another great wordsmith was the Welsh poet, Dylan Thomas, and I see a fairly new-looking copy of 'Under Milk Wood' on your shelves.

That's the replacement copy: I've moved house three times. I've been a Dylan Thomas fan from the beginning as much from hearing the voices in the BBC broadcast which moved me very much. There are passages which move me to tears, from such characters as Reverend Eli Jenkins:

> Every morning when I wake,
> Dear Lord, a little prayer I make.
> O please to keep Thy lovely eye
> On all poor creatures born to die.
>
> We are not wholly bad or good
> Who live our lives under Milk Wood.
> And Thou I know will be the first
> To see our best side not our worst.

I can still remember the first time I heard the voices in *Under Milk Wood* and, contrary to many of the things said later, I would assert the craftsmanship of Dylan Thomas. There has been a very hostile school of criticism that I lived with in the the late '60s and early '70s that thought there was some great Celtic flaw in writers such as Dylan Thomas and Brendan Behan, but I regard them very highly as superb craftsmen.

Moving along your shelves I see a volume entitled 'The Denial of Death' by Earnest Becker, a Pulitzer Prize-winner from 1974.

Becker died just after writing this book, and what fascinated me about it was that it appeared as if he knew he was dying, because the book is an attempt to say something significant. He is looking back through the psychoanalytical tradition and he goes back before Freud to Kierkegaard. He raises a fundamental question that we are struck with a terrible duality: we are animal and sexed and therefore share the basic instinct of all animals for survival; and at the same time we are godlike in our ability to use symbols. He moves on to question a second birth beyond repression. Is it because we are repressed that there can be, as Norman Brown suggests, a second birth beyond repression in which our repression is thrown away and we would be better and freer? Becker rejects this and his stand is that this would leave you psychotic. So then, if we are to choose repressions of some sort, our sovereignty is in the choice of these repressions. Most importantly, the suggestion coming through is that we live with one form of illusion or another and that in the flux between illusions we can only steer in what we think is the direction of the miracle that will come: the revelatory moment of our humanness and our humanity. These moments of ecstasy come, and the interesting fact is that the man was writing the book in the months before he died. It is a beautifully accessible book and an introduction straight back though the analytic tradition to Kierkegaard.

Here's a volume that was a great cult hit in the 1960s and part of that whole hippy generation. It's Hermann Hesse's novel 'Siddartha'.

A couple of things interested me about his – I got presents of four separate copies of *Steppenwolf* and one copy of *Siddartha* – I wonder if someone was trying to tell me something. I loved *Siddartha* always, particularly for Govinda's position. I love parts of this book that were so beautiful and so reflective. Siddartha at one point says, 'When somebody is seeking it happens quite easily that he only sees the thing that he is seeking, that he is unable to find anything, unable to absorb anything because he is only thinking of the thing he is seeking because he has a goal, because he is obsessed with his goal.'

I like the rigid nature of the conclusion of *Siddartha* – it doesn't make the concessions of some of the softer literature. I like reading it now in the 1990s as a celebration of the beauty and the courage and the heroism of the space of life between certainties. Siddartha says, 'You know, my friend, that even as a young man when we lived with the ascetics in the forest I came to distrust doctrines and teachers and to turn my back on them. I am still of the same turn of mind.' There is a warning in it still that the most beautiful thing you have, the most divine thing a person has, is their creative impulse and their imagination. So in a way this question of the integrity of imagination and an imagination that cannot be defeated and to imagine, not for oneself, but for all humanity better shapes and systems, including economic and social and political systems – that is the finest thing that we possess.

32

FINTAN O' TOOLE

Fintan O'Toole was born in Dublin where he is a columnist with *The Irish Times*. He has written widely on politics, current affairs and the arts. He was theatre critic for *In Dublin* and later for *The Sunday Tribune*. He edited *Magill* magazine and in 1993 won the A. T. Cross Irish Journalist of the Year Award. He has written *The Politics of Magic* on the Theatre of Tom Murphy, *No More Heroes – A Radical Guide to Shakespeare* and two volumes of essays, *A Mass for Jesse James* and *Black Hole, Green Card*. His most recent publication is an acclaimed study of the Irish Beef Tribunal, *Meanwhile Back at the Ranch*. He is a constant broadcaster on radio and television, and has presented the BBC television *Late Show*.

Fintan O'Toole, columnist, critic and author, were you brought up in a house of books?

I was very fortunate in that, although neither of my parents had the benefit of a great deal of schooling, they were both readers, my father in particular. Most of the books were kept in the attic and there was always a difficulty in getting them down to read them. I remember my wife telling me, when we were going out together and before she met my father, that she had seen my father, who was a bus conductor, on her way to work. I asked her how she knew it was my father and she replied that he was the only bus conductor she ever saw reading Camus. So I was very lucky growing up in that books were just part of the household.

A book I see on your shelves here has been very formative in your thinking. It's 'Das Kapital' by Karl Marx. What age were you when you first read that?

I was fifteen years of age in the Christian Brothers' School studying for the Intermediate Certificate when I first read *Das Kapital*. I had a vague notion that all the unhappiness of the world and feelings of being put upon could be explained by reading Karl Marx. Myself and some friends in the class saved up fifty pence each and we bought it in the Communist Party Bookshop. Of course, the most terrible shock in your life that you ever get at fifteen is when you expect this book is going to help you get at the Christian Brothers. *Das Kapital* is full of the formula for the conversion of surplus value into production value. It's a very dense textbook but reading it was the first time I had ever encountered something so completely out of my own world, whose concepts, whose ways of thinking were so foreign and so difficult. I probably didn't understand a word of it but I felt I had to read it and it probably did me good in the long run. There was a sense, at fifteen, that maybe this book could change your life and in some ways maybe it did. The great thing about Marx as a popular writer who was widely read was of course that he brought with him the whole sweep of classical philosophy, of Hegel and the whole tradition of the Romantic movement. Marx is a very unfashionable figure nowadays, but what people forget about him is that he is a wonderful writer who was a great poet in many ways. I think he will live as a writer long after his direct ideas have ceased to have relevance.

The theatre is another passion of yours, and you have Kenneth Tynan, the English critic's, volume 'He Who Plays the King' on your shelves. Do you rate him as a great critic?

For years, when I was writing theatre criticism I refused to read Tynan because I was afraid they would say, 'Oh he's only a poor man's Kenneth Tynan!' I came across this first book of his in Kenny's Bookshop in Galway. It was published in 1960 when Tynan was about twenty-five, and it is one of those books that would make you sick, it's so good. It's simply a kind of diary of watching the great Shakespearian performances in the late '40s and early '50s, which happened to coincide with the great period of Olivier, Gielgud, Richardson: the great Shakespearian actors were doing the great roles. Tynan I find really interesting: he is someone whose ideas you may or may not share but you cannot deny the power of the writing. There's a sense of life in his writing, a wonderful sense of someone who was prepared to change his views as he got older. In this book Tynan is very conservative in his view of the theatre, but he became much more radical in the 1960s and tried to discard his old self. Maybe this is the sort of book that is good for the victims of critics where you can drag it out and say to the critic, 'Well you didn't think this way ten years ago!' I suppose what Tynan did for theatre criticism was to bring it back to the sense of presence, about being there in the theatre and what happens between those four walls on the night.

I suppose you could describe the next book I see here as 'The Cynic's Handbook'. It's 'The Devil's Dictionary' by Ambrose Bierce. What appeals to you about this book?

This is a book I literally picked up out of a bin in London when I was a student. Bierce is probably not as well known as he should be, and his *Devil's Dictionary* is full of cynicism, dry humour and a very bleak and black but funny view of the world. It's actually written as a dictionary which defines things for you, and is always completely straight to the point. Opening it at random I see a definition of *future* (noun): 'That period of time in which our affairs prosper, our friends are true and our happiness is self-assured.'

Bierce has always been good for me because I tend to get carried away by things and to have that cynical little voice in the background seeing the funny side is great.

The next book I see is a Pulitzer Prize-winner, and it's a history of the Vietnam war, Neil Sheehan's 'A Bright Shining Lie'.

If you work in journalism you look for books which do something different with the tools of the trade. Sheehan's book is a history of the Vietnam war told through one character, a man called John Paul Vann, who was one of the leading strategists on the American side. What is amazing is that it intermingles huge history in all the trauma and horror of the war and at the same time the story of one man's personal breakdown. The book intermingles his political life and his sex life. The kind of madness that was going on all around him is reflected in his treatment of women and of his family. As a journalist, what you are always trying to do is to bring big things down to a comprehensible and human level. Sheehan's book, as huge and massive as its subject, is a book which holds out a wonderful notion of how you can take a personal line through history and be moved by it. History means more to you in that way than when it is merely a set of facts.

Further down on another shelf I see an 1825 edition of memoirs of the 'Life of the Right Honourable Richard Brindsley Sheridan' by Thomas Moore.

Sheridan is a figure I've become more and more interested in, partly I suppose because we are interested in people who reflect our own interests. Sheridan was both the greatest playwright of his time in the English language, but also the greatest political orator of his day and a very major political figure, which people in Ireland tend to forget. He had become a fascinating figure because he was both Irish and English. He left Dublin where he was born in his teens and spent most of the rest of his life in England but was always a very Irish figure. The book is fascinating because it is written from the perspective of another very double-edged kind of Irish Englishman, Thomas Moore, the ballad and song-writer, who was also trying to get on in England. He too was trying to be famous in London while retaining a sense of his own Irishness. You get a kind of double drama going on in the book: you get Sheridan and his life but you also get Moore trying to reflect on that. It's a book which is old and out of print, which is part of history, and yet when you read it it somehow gives you a very interesting perspective on Ireland now. This is not the first time that we have faced problems about how to be Irish and something else. You realise a lot of very bright Irish people have had to face these questions for a very long time, and there is a certain drama in this book which makes it worth coming back to.

Here's a three-volume work I see on your shelves, called 'The Principles of Hope', by Ernest Bloch.

This is an odd book which seems to me to be one of the great works of the twentieth century. Bloch is a fascinating figure, a German Jewish Marxist, who lost his family fortune in the Russian Revolution but still believed in that movement. The book was written in the United States during the war, when he fled the Nazi persecution, and it's written at perhaps the darkest moment of twentieth-century history, yet it is called *The Principle of Hope*. It is a huge fifteen-hundred-page essay on what are the concrete bases for hope. How do we find hope, where is it? It deals with hope mainly in terms of art with a huge range of reference and of detail going from music to the visual arts to theatre and poetry. These are put into a very broad metaphysical and political context. This book was published in Germany in the early 1950s and it took thirty years to be translated into English because it was big and difficult. I think it is a book which will work its way into English-language consciousness more and more, because at the moment it seems very important since we have lost a sense of hope, and yearn for a sense of change. We have lost a sense of the world as not everything that is the case but, as the poet, Derek Mahon, puts it, the world is also everything "that is thought to be the case," everything we can think and imagine and feel. This is, I suppose, my secular Bible.

Someone I know you greatly admire since your college days is the Scottish poet Hugh McDiarmid, and I see his 'Complete Poems' have pride of place on your shelves. You are still fascinated by that quirky, angular man.

I suppose you realise, if you come out of a political tradition in the way I do, you want things to be one thing or the other. Someone like McDiarmid is a good corrective because he is so contradictory, he is so mad and is perverse in certain ways. In some ways it is good to remember that sometimes the function of art is to be perverse, to just contradict itself. Maybe he was the ultimate thorn in the side; he was a writer who constantly went back on himself and contradicted himself. Politically, he was thrown out of the Scottish National Party which he helped to found for being a communist, and he was then thrown out of the Communist Party for being a Scottish Nationalist. His *Collected Poems* is a masterwork that spans most of the century, and in it you get the sense of a great and perverse mind, a mind at an angle to everything, working its way through the great events of the century. You can almost read it as a secret history of our time.

I suspect the next set of books on your shelves would be your Desert Island choice – 'The Complete Works of Shakespeare'.

When I was thirteen my father told me that by the time he was thirteen he had read the complete works of Shakespeare and everybody did this. So I spent a summer when I was thirteen desperately trying to read the complete works. I think I probably took in almost nothing, but it was the beginning of a lifelong contract with the richness of that whole world. Even a cheap edition of Shakespeare still offers riches beyond cost, and I'll always come back to it.

33

NORA RELIHAN

Nora Relihan, social worker, actress, theatre director and broadcaster, comes from a long line of Kerry ancestry. She was educated in various schools in Kerry, Tipperary and Limerick, and then trained as a nurse in London where she worked in Guys Hospital. Back in Kerry, actor Eamon Kelly introduced her to Listowel Drama Group where she created the role of Mena in John B. Keane's play *Sive* in 1959. That production won the All-Ireland Drama Festival Overall Award and played in Dublin at the Old Queen's Theatre. She subsequently played the role of Mena in Cork, Belfast and Dublin. With John B. Keane she founded the Listowel Players and both played, and directed many of their most successful shows. She has performed a series of one-woman shows based on Irish poetry, drama and literature, including a version of *The Midnight Court*. She was a member of the Arts Council from 1979 to 1983, President of Listowel Writers' Week and Chairperson of St John's Listowel Arts Centre since 1987. She is also a drama adjudicator and regular broadcaster with Radio Kerry.

We're about a mile outside Listowel in the home of Nora Relihan, actress, President of Listowel Writers' Week and broadcaster. Given your lifelong interest in the theatre, it's no surprise to find you have the autobiography of American playwright, Arthur Miller, called 'Timebends', on your shelves.

The man is special to me because he is such a brilliant playwright. I first came in contact with his plays in 1974 when I helped to direct and performed in *The Crucible* with the Listowel Players. There are many reasons why *The Crucible* is special to me – one of them is that it got me involved in St John's Arts and Heritage Centre in Listowel Square. The hymn that we used in that production of *The Crucible* was rehearsed in St John's Church as the fair day sounds drifted in from the town mixed with the swell of the organ played by the Archdeacon. The sunlight was streaming in through the stained-glass window and I fell in love with St John's and that affair has continued. I thought *The Crucible* was so interesting because Miller was not afraid to select a microcosm of American life, in this case exploring McCarthyism, relating the New England Salem witch trials to the contemporary situation in the United States in the 1950s. It was an inverse parable in that the modern witch hunt under McCarthy was explored in terms of the old story of hysteria in Salem. All of Miller's plays reflect a man who knew himself, who was sure of himself in his Jewish roots and his unashamedness about his poor background and where he came from. I admire his confidence in himself because I recall when I was nursing in a very snobby hospital in London, England, I remember thinking some of my colleagues had so much more than I had and I felt inhibited talking about my background in the face of these colonial types and minor aristocrats. When you read a book like this it enhances your sense of your own worth and gives you renewed confidence in yourself and your roots.

Another man of the theatre who had a controversial life was Richard Burton, and you have his biography by Melvyn Bragg. You were in love with Burton.

Burton was great. I don't know if I was in love with him, but you would have to love his voice. It's the kind of voice that for its distinctiveness and beauty is reminiscent of the late Eamon Keane. I loved both their voices. Reading about Burton you realise he was a man of colour and hyperbole. You can't think of Burton without thinking of Elizabeth Taylor and the fact that he and she were in the theatre and films together and they were married to each other twice. Burton burned himself out and had a great self-destructive urge, which gave you a feeling he was definitely a fellow Celt.

Burton was a wonderful performer of poetry and that brings us to a new edition on your shelves of Palgrave's 'Golden Treasury'.

I love this anthology and I'd like to read one of my favourite poems from it, by Robert Herrick.

To the Virgins, To Make Much of Time

Gather ye rose-buds while ye may,
Old Time is still a-flying:

And this same flower that smiles today,
Tomorrow will be dying.

The glorious lamp of heaven, the Sun,
The higher he's a getting;
The sooner will his race be run,
And nearer he's to setting.

That age is best, which is the first,
When youth and blood are warmer;
But being spent, the worse, and worst
Times, still succeed the former.

Then be not coy, but use your time;
And while ye may, go marry:
For having lost but once your prime,
You may for every tarry.

You also have a lot of contemporary poetry on your shelves and you are particularly fond of the work of Nuala Ní Dhomhnaill, which you have performed in your shows.

I think that Nuala Ní Dhomhnaill is not afraid to be a sensual woman and she can express herself without self-consciousness totally as a woman. We have as women often felt so censored in this country by a puritanical Jansenistic relic of old times, which has caused our souls sometimes to shrivel up, and denied us the right to enjoy ourselves fully as people. Nuala speaks for people like me and she has the temper of a redhead too, of course. She was born in England but raised in Ireland and is a native Irish speaker. Later, she had the courage to go off to Turkey and make her life there. She is very much her own woman.

Someone who was very much his own man was Patrick Kavanagh and your copy of his 'Collected Poems' looks well thumbed. You have a favourite few lines from Kavanagh engraved in a special place in your house.

They're written over the bath in my bathroom! It's from his poem 'Memory of Brother Michael'.

Culture is always something that was,
Something pedants can measure,
Skull of bard, thigh of chief,
Depths of dried-up river.
Shall we be thus forever?
Shall we be thus forever?

I went on a pilgrimage recently to Inishkeen, Kavanagh country in Monaghan, and I committed a bit of thieving. I crept in under Kananagh's barn in Mucker and stole a chipped enamel basin. Someone said it must have been under his bed. I have it here and I'm going to set flowers in it and call it Kavanagh's Bed.

Not all the books on your shelves are poetic or theatrical. You have some books by Dick Francis about the horse world – here's one called 'Long Shot'.

I like Dick Francis because there's a bonus in the fact that they are both thrillers and set in the horsey world. I was brought up in a house and within a family that were very involved with horses in one way or another. I don't know anything about horses: I don't ride but I like watching them run and we have a very big race meeting in Listowel very year. When we took a play of John B. Keane, which I directed, on tour to London I said I'd go because it gave me the opportunity to go to Cheltenham Races for a day. Side by side with Dick Francis I have another great contemporary English writer – John Mortimer and his *Rumpole of the Bailey* stories. I think there is a certain element of the old reprobate about both Rumpole and his creator John Mortimer. They are both people who have lived. Brendan Kennelly said to me recently as we were sitting in Siamsa Tíre at a show in Tralee, looking up at a woman performing on stage, 'You know, Nora, you can't beat a woman who has lived!' I feel the same about Rumpole and Mortimer – they both have a great sense of having lived in the world and enjoyed themselves.

One of the most interesting Irish political autobiographies of recent years was Noel Browne's 'Against the Tide'. He is someone you've admired over the years.

I've admired him very much, although I might not agree with all his views. I think it is very necessary in political life and in the life of the country to have people who rock the boat. I think people like Noel Browne, with ideals they are prepared to stand over, cause society to improve. He is a wonderful man.

We can't finish without a few lines from your favourite poet, William Butler Yeats. What have you chosen?

I would like to read 'The Heart of the Woman'.

> O what to me the little room
> That was brimmed up with prayer and rest;
> He bade me out into the gloom,
> And my breast lies upon his breast.
>
> O what to me my mother's care,
> The house where I was safe and warm;
> The shadowy blossom of my hair
> Will hide us from the bitter storm.
>
> O hiding hair and dewy eyes,
> I am no more with life and death,
> My heart upon his warm heart lies,
> My breath is mixed into his breath.

34

BRENDAN KENNELLY

Brendan Kennelly, Professor of English Literature at Trinity College, Dublin, poet, playwright and novelist, was born in Ballylongford, County Kerry. He was educated at Trinity College and Leeds University. He has lectured widely abroad and was Cornell Professor of Literature in Swarthmore College, Pennsylvania from 1971 to 1972. He has published over twenty books of poems including *My Dark Fathers* (1964), *Good Souls to Survive* (1968), *Shelley in Dublin* (1974), *The House that Jack Didn't Build* (1982) and two long poem sequences, *Cromwell* (1983) and *Judas* (1991). He has translated widely from the Irish language and his translations are now collected in a volume called *Love of Ireland: Poems from the Irish* and he has edited *The Penguin Book of Irish Verse*. He has written two novels, *The Crooked Cross* and *The Florentines,* and for the theatre he has written versions of *Antigone* and *Medea*. He is a popular broadcaster and performer of his work.

Brendan Kennelly, poet and professor, the first book I see on your shelves was written by an old teacher of yours here in Trinity College. It's Alec Reid's book on the works of Samuel Beckett, 'All I Can Manage, More than I Could'.

When I started studying English here in Trinity, Alec Reid was one of my teachers. He was a fascinating figure – a small chubby man with white hair and a terrific voice. He used no notes when he was giving a lecture and he would quote poems by heart. He would turn you on to people like T. S. Eliot and Ezra Pound and all the Moderns, and then he could go back to the Metaphysical and Romantic poets and he would take you trotting through all the phases of literature in one lecture. Throughout his life he showed an enormous interest in Samuel Beckett, and I know that he went to Paris to meet him. There have been so many books about Beckett that it is intimidating to read through even the bibliography about him. Yet this little book, published by the Dolmen Press, is one of my favourite books about Beckett and was written many years ago. Alec

Reid is dead now, God rest him, and he has left this little gem of a book behind him which I cherish most of all. In it he brings alive Beckett the character and the kind of mind he had. He talks about about his genius for companionship, the remarkable ability he had to make those who came in contact with him feel the richer for his mere presence. He quotes somebody who says about Beckett, 'Sam is the sort of person you could wander off with and watch rats swimming in the river and you'd both feel you'd spent a useful afternoon.' Reid picks out this work 'both' because Beckett always imparts this sense of something shared, of someone coming along with you. Now that's very against the way people often write about Beckett, that he is totally isolated, a man of despair, a man who feels and can impart nothing but the desolation of reality. I think that is there but it is almost how you read Beckett, how you listen to him – and the way Alec Reid could listen to him and read him meant that he could steal the warmth of Beckett's heart and transmit it to his students. So I grew up thinking of Beckett as a warm comic writer in the way Reid taught him to us, and I've never lost that and I often say to people when they are facing the intellectual complexity of this great writer, 'Enjoy his laughter.' He tells great stories too about Beckett and Brendan Behan. One story about Behan, whom Beckett liked very much, goes like so: Behan, in Paris found himself under lock and key due to some temporary financial embarrassment. Beckett heard about Behan's plight and sought him out. Then in Behan's words he recalls, 'Beckett paid them what I owed them and he took me away and he gave me ten thousand francs and a double brandy and a lecture on the evils of drinking!' Alec Reid adds, 'A nicer sense of priorities would be hard to imagine.' It shows again the wonderful humanity of Beckett in helping Behan who was, of course, such a wonderfully humane writer. It's funny how over the years some books stick with you, and this one has stayed with me, this book of a teacher who has long gone to his reward.

A woman for whom have you have had a great admiration over the years is Simone Weil, and her book 'Gravity and Grace' impressed you greatly.

Well, it's a very difficult book and I'm not saying that I understand it although I have read it dozens and dozens of times. First of all she is a mystical writer. She is a young Jewish woman born in Paris in 1909 and she died towards the end of the Second World War when her own Jewish people were being annihilated by Hitler. She took it on herself to feel what they felt: she fasted with them, she prayed for them, she thought about them. She worked in the vineyard of France doing men's work, punishing her body and disciplining her mind. I suppose it's something we would all like to do, but at least you can admire it when you see it in another. She is moving always between Judaism and Christianity in term of ideas and in terms of connecting them. It's a fascinating journey from the Judaic Old Testament into the Christian New Testament and then throughout the centuries to follow the ways in which men and women interpret these two great systems but in so doing have defined often their own smallness of spirit. The result is that the beauty of Judaism and the beauty of Christianity have never been bought together, and I think that Simone Weil united these two great traditions. She is shockingly epigrammatical. Her God is distant, austere, not easy to understand. She glorifies suffering and she is very given to punishing the mind. The result for me, as a limited reader of her work, is that I find she helps me with my teaching. You read, in a sense, to help you with your life and my life is part teaching and part writing. When I read Simone Weil I understand something like paying attention, for example. There is a great phrase in an old German poem quoted by Yeats somewhere: 'God asks nothing of the highest soul but attention.' Now, in this day and age, research has been done to say that the common attention span of the average American is eight seconds. Because of television, because of the availability of things, the sense of which we want to be entertained, amused, informed without working for it, without paying attention, are all pervasive. Simone Weil comes along and says:

> The poet produces the beautiful by fixing his attention on
> something real. It is the same with the act of love. To know
> that this man who is hungry and thirsty really exists as much
> as I do – that is enough, the rest follows of itself. The
> authentic and pure values – truth, beauty and goodness – in
> the activity of a human being are the result of one and the
> same act, a certain application of the full attention to the

object. Teaching should have no aim but to prepare, by training the attention, for the possibility of such an act.

All the other advantages of instruction are without interest. She is very absolutist but she tells you to transfer to students a sense of their potential for paying attention to the work in hand.

You have a small Oxford book here with a lovely green cover, an anthology called 'Dublin' by Benedict Kiely.

I love it and I read very often this anthology compiled by Ben Kiely. Kiely is a great storyteller, a very gifted novelist, an extraordinary writer of short stories, and a very good broadcaster. He is a writer whose work has been consistent and abundant, and I'm glad to have the opportunity to say that this man, together with John Millington Synge, in the best writer about places around Ireland that I have read. His anthology about Dublin is a delight. It is a small book but it goes right through the city and it is the book of a stroller. Somebody once said that Dublin is a city for strolling through and I can vouch for that, because sometimes I don't sleep very well and I get up in the morning and walk around the city, choosing whatever area I like, and go and look at it at five o'clock on a summer or autumn morning. Then I see anywhere from Rathmines or Rathgar out to Clontarf and I can go out in any direction. That is the kind of dream sauntering yet precise and documented anthology about Dublin that Ben Kiely has given us. He starts with a little story:

> During the Hitler war when transport with many other matters was in trouble, a citizen complained bitterly that he was not allowed onto the last bus out of town on a certain route. He had family pride and he said 'I am one of the Glenns of Kilbarrack and I insist on boarding this bus.' And the conductor said, 'Sir, if you were one of the Glens of Antrim I still couldn't fit youse in.'

The story illustrates the wit and wisdom of Dublin. A woman who embodied that spirit was Kathleen Behan, and I see you have 'Mother of All the Behans', the autobiography of Kathleen Behan as told to her son Brian Behan.

I love this book and Rosaleen Linehan's interpretation of it is a classic piece of theatre. It is to me a tribute to a woman who knew hardship and suffering and at the same time preserved her greatness of spirit, her ability to sing and her ability to put things in context. She never let herself go down and I know that's very hard. It's very difficult to keep yourself afloat if things are hitting you from within and without. God knows this woman had it really tough. She describes how she was in the city in Russell Street with all the children and then moving out into the suburbs. Of course she is wonderful about her son Brendan. She describes his imprisonment in England and how he came back, how he got into trouble and it was said he was going to be shot on sight. She's a great woman – she lasted and and survived and she sang.

You have a book of poems by a very special person you loved dearly. It's Davoren Hanna's 'Not Common Speech', published by the Raven Arts Press.

This boy was disabled and he had a great mother, Brid Hanna, who died a few years ago quite young. She literally gave life to him. Then he died a couple of years ago after his poems had been collected and published by Dermot Bolger. I'd like to finish by reading one of his poems which says it all.

> The moon blackened at my birth
> and long night's cry began.
> Pain became my bed-fellow
> and despair my song.
> God disappeared behind the clouds;
> I lost my star-signpost to hope.

> Light found a chink to peep though
> when poems were read to my starved soul.
> Loneliness brought moments of repose;
> lines poured through my veins

and love glimmered on my tongue.
Little birds became my inspiration.

Left with my own silent melody,
I painted notes of long-forgotten tunes
trembling in my trapped heart.
Light burst through my dark mouth.
and myriad songs flew heavenwards.
I was poised for flight...

35

MARY LELAND

Mary Leland was born and reared in Cork where she was encouraged to write by her English teacher Miss O'Sullivan, who was instrumental in suggesting that she join *The Cork Examiner* as a journalist. After spending some years in Dublin she returned to Cork as a freelance writer, mainly for *The Irish Times*. Her first short stories were published by David Marcus in the *Irish Press*, and in 1980 she won the Listowel Writers' Week Short Story Award. Her first novel, *The Killeen*, was published in 1985, and in 1987 she published *The Little Galloway Girls*. Her 1991 novel, *Approaching Priests*, is set in a post-Vatican II Ireland coming to terms with being European and modern.

We're in the very pleasant Cork suburb of Blackrock, overlooking the River Lee, and I'm in the home of author and journalist, Mary Leland, surrounded by books. I notice you have a penchant for the Victorian novelists like Mrs Elizabeth Gaskill, for example.

I suppose it comes from the wonderful experience some of us had of having an education that made absolutely sure that were familiar with the works of Jane Austin and the Brontës, whether we wanted to or not. It has left me with a great affection for Jane Austen and the Brontës but it also made me a little bit curious about people like Elizabeth Gaskill after reading her *Life of Charlotte Brontë* which, despite all its flaws, is one of the best biographies ever written. In the edition I have of *The Life of Charlotte Brontë* there was a biographical note about the author Elizabeth Gaskill, and I just had to go on and find all I could about her and the best way is to read her work. I read all her novels. I didn't relish all of them, because some of them are quite tough. She was an extraordinary woman for a Victorian in that she did try to tackle very unpopular social issues of her day, unpopular certainly in terms of women writers. I think her prose is classical. Even though she was dealing with very contemporary issues the style of her writing is undeviating and absolutely beautiful. So I do indulge myself with a good Gaskill novel, of which there are only four or five because she was not very prolific. As for the softer side of Victorian fiction, I enjoy Anthony Trollope and I have read as many of his novels as I could possible lay my hands on. I like *The Belton Estate* because, although Trollope was very fond of describing the upper echelons of British society, in this novel he was very clear-cut about the role of women in that society. His heroine, Clara, is a study of what happens to women who have no income and of how important marriage is in those circumstances. I think we are very inclined to forget that a woman's marriageability in all levels of society was not just the stuff of fiction but the stuff of real life in a horribly pertinent way. Trollope has terrific plots in his novels but he does deal with very serious elements of society, in a way that I find very exciting. Mrs Oliphant, another writer, is an example of the kind of woman Trollope was writing about. She was a woman who had to support herself and her husband and her extended family by her pen. She considered herself a rival of Trollope in that she couldn't understand why he was so popular and so well known and so highly regarded and she wasn't. The real reason was that she had to write for a living in the frantic way while he was earning a very good living from the British Post Office before he gave up his job and became a full-time writer. She produced hundreds of stories and novels, not many of which have survived now, but Mrs Oliphant at her best is well worth reading, and even at her worst I have an affection for her because she was such a grafter.

Many people have discovered her novels like *Chronicles of Carlingford* in Virago Classics which have re-issued her work.

An Irish writer I see on your shelves who was popular in the 1940s and '50s is Maura Laverty.

I don't remember her being hugely popular when I was growing up. I remember Annie M. P. Smithson as a sort of demon in female flesh and very popular. I wonder if Maura Laverty was really popular in her day – I think novels like *Never No More* are more talked about today. The first book by Maura Laverty that ever came into my hands was her cookery book *Full and Plenty,* and it was from there that I moved on to her novels *No More than Human* and *Never No More. No More than Human* was about that wonderful fashion in Irish life in the 1930s and '40s where young Irish girls were sent off to Spain as governesses, almost in the Kate O'Brien tradition. As an Irish writer I think Maura Laverty is underrated because she was full of humour and insight into humanity.

Here's a book which is probably out of print now, 'Sweet Cork of Thee' by Robert Gibbings.

I think this was the first book I came across that showed me that my own city of Cork had lyrical potential. He was a journeyman artist who travelled a great deal and has written books about the South Sea Islands and one about England, called *Sweet Thames Flow Softly*. His other Cork book is called *Lovely Is the Lee*. He writes about people he meets and places he goes in Cork city and especially in West Cork around Gougane Barra and the characters he meets there. It's a very attractive book, beautifully produced by J. M. Dent in London in 1952, with wonderful woodcuts, and I'm very lucky to have his two books about Cork.

Here's a Penguin Modern Classic – Ford Madox Ford's 'Memories and Impressions', a kind of ragbag of a book full of essays, anecdotes and autobiographical extracts taken from all over his work.

This is a wonderful instruction to Ford Madox Ford. I find myself having a great admiration for those writers who stuck to their best and who day after day kept on writing, writing, writing. Inevitably some of their writing wasn't marvellous, but I find Ford had a steady standard. He was interested in the achievement of a really good writing style. His anecdotes about visiting Henry James, where he imitates James's hyphenated bracketed style were marvellous. I found Ford's *Memories and Impressions* a great way of meeting other artists and writers whose biographies perhaps often don't do them justice. We get a glimpse of them in a very immediate and living sense through Ford, and in a way I relish and admire.

Here's another Penguin paperback which you have well thumbed. It's Angus Wilson's 'No Laughing Matter' which is described as a chronicle of the last fifty-five years as reflected in the fortunes of a London middle-class family. Is it very funny?

The first half of this novel is very funny if you like his slightly distant acerbic view of life and I do. *No Laughing Matter* is funny but very bitter and sad at the end. This was the first Angus Wilson I read and it was a great discovery to find there are all those books of his yet to be read.

If there is a consistent thread through the books you have chosen to talk about it's the question of style. You really do admire prose stylists and writers who write stylishly and elegantly.

I do, and I must say that I find, with a few general exceptions, women seem to do it best of all. That may be a generalisation but look at the biographical writings of Victoria Glendinning or Ruth Dudley Edwards. These women write absolutely beautifully but nobody gives them credit for it. I admire persistence and I admire style in writing – two lynchpins for me.

36

SEAN J. WHITE

Sean J. White was born in Durrow, County Laois and educated at University College, Cork, University College, Dublin and Oxford. He lectured in Maynooth College and UCD. He joined the *Irish Press* in 1958 where, with Ben Kiely, he wrote the daily Patrick Lagan column, and was assistant literary editor and theatre critic. From 1965 he was Senior Public Relations Officer with Bord Fáilte, and later Publicity Director North America until 1971. He then became Head of Information with Coras Iompar Éireann until 1977. From 1980 to 1989 he was Dean of the School of Irish Studies, and he is currently Director of Irish Studies Programme and Professor in the University of Limerick. He has published short stories in *The Bell* magazine, edited *Irish Writing* from 1954 to 1958 and has been a frequent broadcaster on radio and television. He has been a long-serving member of the Committee of Cumann Merriman, and has directed three of their summer schools.

Laoisman, scholar, journalist, lecturer and inveterate book collector, Sean J. White, can you remember what was the first book you bought with your own money?

At first, I remember I had books bought for me – the usual boy's books and school annuals – although in Durrow, County Laois where I grew up it was pretty difficult to buy books and one depended on swapping books. The first book I actually paid money for was when I was at secondary school in St Kiernan's College in Kilkenny. It was a battered edition of Sir Walter Scott's *Ivanhoe* and I bought it from a chap called Martin Ryan for one and sixpence. In my youth I think I was a snob about reading because someone put the idea into my head that I should read the classics. I remember we were lucky in Durrow in that we had a circulating library run by a Miss O'Rourke, who had a great collection of the classics. I started reading Charles Dickens there, and later I started buying Dickens and Scott because I thought they were the right books to read. Other fellows might be buying cowboy books at that time. My first real book-buying was in Dublin with the great resources of Webbs on the

Quays and Greenes in Clare Street where you could buy most classics for about one and sixpence. That's when I began seriously collecting books. I was able to buy some rare editions, although at the time the money was rare too. I remember one particular volume I bought in Cork. When I was at university there I had the lucky job of being librarian at St Patrick's Hostel and that gave me access to the bookshops. I remember the Lee Bookshop on the Quay run by Mr McSweeney and from him I bought, for the enormous sum of nine shillings, an edition of Jeremiah Callanan's *Poems* and when I looked into it I found I had an unknown edition of his poems. Normally it was said his first book of poems was published in 1828. The one I had was unknown and published in 1829, by which time Jeremiah Callanan was dead. That was my first bibliophile item all those years ago.

Because of your involvement in the Irish literary world over the years you have many books by friends on your shelves. Would it be invidious to ask you to make a selection from them?

Many of my friends are dead and won't complain, and the others shouldn't worry. I was lucky when I came to Dublin at the beginning of the 1950s that I got into literary circles. I was doing an MA thesis at the time. I got to know people like Austin Clarke, M. J. McManus, Cathal O'Shannon, and through them I got to know living novelists like Benedict Kiely, who remains a firm friend of mine and a favourite author. I think I have an edition of everything he ever wrote. Francis MacManus, who was from the neighbouring county of Kilkenny, features on my shelves, as does Mervyn Wall. I also have almost everything written by people I met afterwards like Edna O'Brien, John Broderick and John McGahern. To collect the works of Seán O'Faolain and Frank O'Connor was extremely difficult because their works were banned when they came out.

You have here full collections of some of the literary magazines of the 1940s, '50s and '60s. They must be quite valuable by now.

Yes, but of course nowadays a lot of them are printed in reproductions. I succeeded David Marcus as editor of *Irish Writing* in 1954, and I have the full run of that magazine. *The Bell* of course was the great bible for our generation and it's on the top shelf up there. There too are *Envoy* magazine, which was edited by John Ryan, and *Threshold* magazine from Belfast, edited by Mary O'Malley. One of my favourites was *The Kilkenny Magazine,* edited by James Delahunty in the 1960s, from Kilkenny which published, for the first time in Ireland, people like Seamus Heaney and John McGahern.

The mention of Kilkenny brings us to a famous book here on your shelves – Canon Carrigan's 'History of the Diocese of Ossory', in three volumes.

That is probably a paradigm of my whole book collecting. Canon Carrigan, the historian of the Diocese of Ossory, was parish priest of my native Durrow in County Laois just before I was born. He was a very scholarly man and his diocesan history was probably the best that was ever written. When I grew up in Durrow, to possess the Book, as it was known, was a kind of title of nobility; it meant that in 1904, when Carrigan's *History* was published, your people had two guineas to spend. Now my people were not in Durrow but wherever they were in Laois they obviously hadn't two guineas to spend, because they are not in the list of subscriptions. I always wanted to get that book. I once saw it go up for sale for twelve guineas and I didn't have twelve guineas at the time. Then it came up for auction in the mid 1960s and my wife, while reading the paper next morning, said, 'I see you didn't get the Carrigan.' I asked her how she knew and she said, 'It went for twenty-six guineas.' Shocking her somewhat I told her I had bought it. The next edition I bought cost two hundred pounds and the last edition was presented by me by my friend, Don Roberts, who republished it in two volumes in the early '80s in a marvellous edition. So that is how I came to have three sets of Carrigan's *History of the Diocese of Ossory.*

You have many other books here on local history, topography and archaeology, all great interests of yours.

I have a particular interest in the topography, archaeology and local history of County Clare as well as that of my own native County Laois.

I have a particular interest in the Clare poet Brian Merriman, who in the eighteenth century wrote his famous comic epic *The Midnight Court*, a very long poem and a very elegant and erotic poem. That little-known volume is the first printed edition of *The Midnight Court* printed in Angelsea Street in Dublin by John O'Daly in 1840. It had been around in manuscript form since Merriman completed it in the 1780s or so. It has gone through various editions since and many translations too. There are famous translations by Arland Ussher, Lord Longford and a Frank O'Connor version which caused *The Midnight Court* to be banned. More recently, we have fine translations by Thomas Kinsella and David Marcus. No translation can reproduce the spirit of the original – there are horses for courses. O'Connor's is a very brash translation, very bawdy and very lively, and it is the one I would give to people who didn't know Irish and had never read it before. I think Arland Ussher's translation is the more scholarly and I think Thomas Kinsella's recent translation is very satisfactory. None of them have captured exactly in translation the sprightliness and polish of the original, that high elegant veneer of Merriman's eighteenth-century Irish original.

Moving along to the next shelf I see a full collection of the works of the novelist Standish O'Grady, a figure who is neglected these days.

He has gone through various phases of neglect. He was neglected when I started working on him for my MA thesis. I got to know O'Grady's son, so I have not just the printed works but also a collection of letters and memorabilia of O'Grady. He was a pioneer who inspired people like Yeats and Æ in a literary sense and also in a social sense. I find him quite fascinating as a writer. He may come back into fashion again just like the Banim Brothers from Kilkenny who are neglected nineteenth-century novelists. The Banim Brothers, John and Michael, were particularly good novelists. John Banim started his literary career by writing a three-act tragedy and by going to London to try and flog it where he got into company with Gerald Griffin, who had gone there with a similar sort of literary ambition earlier on. His brother, Michael, who stayed at home in Kilkenny running a shop and acting as postmaster, tended to supply the material for the novels. It was a very strange literary collaboration between those two brothers. Their early writings were rather highly coloured imitations of Sir Walter Scott. Then John died and Michael continued on writing in a more realistic but perhaps more turgid way. They give wonderfully atmospheric portrayals of Ireland in the early part of the nineteenth century, pre-Famine, and they reflect the solid life of a county that was Irish-speaking until just around their lifetimes. The people then spoke a sort of English dialect of Irish. The Banim brothers do not deserve to be forgotten, because they occupy an important place in the development of the Anglo-Irish novel, chronicling the transition of the focus of the Irish novel from the Big House to the more ordinary but no less colourful peasant Irish.

37

BOB QUINN

Bob Quinn has been based in Carraroe in Connemara where he works as a film maker and author. Among his best known films are *Atlantean, Cloch, Budwanny, Caoineadh Art Ui Laoghaire, Poitín* and *The Bishop's Story*. He was a television producer in the early days of RTE and in 1969 co-authored the book *Sit Down and Be Counted* with Lelia Doolan and Jack Dowling. He has published articles, stories and poems over many years. His books include *Atlantean: Ireland's North Africa and Maritime Heritage* and *Smokey Hollow*, a memoir of growing up in Dublin. He is a member of Aosdana and a recently appointed member of the RTE Authority.

Carraroe in County Galway is where Bob Quinn, film maker, author, one-time fisherman, broadcaster, photographer, journalist and man of many parts, has come to live over twenty years ago. In the process of your many house moves, have you lost a lot of books?

Of course I have – I've dropped them all over the place leaving a trail like a snail. The biggest bulk of books I lost was when I was living in London in 1969 and I had boxes of books. When I was coming back to snag turnips on Clare Island I left them all behind and I felt guilty because I felt like I was leaving my children behind. I've been here now for twenty years in this house and the books I've accumulated in that period are here. I'm not possessive about books because I've loaned too many, but oddly enough as I grow older I've grown crankier, so now I tend to write down to whom I've loaned books because it's very difficult to get them back.

One book I know that has been a seminal influence on you is T. S. Eliot's 'The Waste Land'. Is that a poem that goes back to your student days or did you come to it later in life?

Well, I was never a formal student in the sense that you are talking about. Indeed, I didn't become aware of the existence of T. S. Eliot until a pal of mine began quoting him down in Brittas Bay where we were camping. I immediately dashed off and got *The Waste Land* and I was staggered by the way the poet's words equated to my perception. I think it's something to do with some kind of depressed or alienated view of reality or of life or society, and he seemed to express or articulate for me the way I saw things. Indeed, not for the first time in my life, I thought, 'I wish I'd written that.' Eliot has been with me for years now. The first time I ever made a film, a training film, I actually tried to make a film of *The Love Song of J. Alfred Prufrock*. I had two middle-aged actors on Killiney beach spouting the lines and had Prufrock rolling up the legs of his trousers and declaring 'Do I dare to eat a peach?'

Philip Larkin might appear to be a natural heir to T. S. Eliot, and I see you have here Larkin's 'Collected Poems'.

Philip Larkin I came across by a friend on Clare Island giving me a present of a copy of his volume *Whitsun Wedding*. Again, I found that Larkin with his ironic and sad view of life appealed to me. He is not a cynic but he doesn't seem to get a lot of joy out of life. What I like about him is his down-to-earth uncompromising statement of reality as in his most famous poem, 'This Be the Verse'.

> They fuck you up, your mum and dad.
> They may not mean to, but they do.
> They fill you with the faults they had
> And add some extra, just for you.

Then there's that terribly depressing last verse:

> Man hands on misery to man.
> It deepens like a coastal shelf.
> So get out as early as you can,
> And don't have any kids yourself.

Maybe Larkin hits on something: that the idea we are one large jolly happy community is far from the truth and that we don't communicate effectively. Maybe people who work in the arts don't talk to each other enough and we don't actually know that we exist in the same alienated sense.

*You have a well-battered copy of Herbert Marcuse's 'One-dimensional Man –
The Ideology of Industrial Society' and that too is a book that helped shape your
thinking.*

That's a kind of bible for me. I'm glad you didn't look inside the cover
because it says 'RTE Reference Library', and it's one of the things I
brought with me from RTE when I left in 1969. Marcuse in the 1960s,
in his Californian university, pointed out that all protest in our capitalist
society, including anarchy, used to have some kind of effect but now all
protest is absorbed by our amazing system. Indeed that is probably the
most depressing book I've ever read and I tend to read it to find out some
flaw in his philosophy but I think he is right: protest is absorbed by the
capitalist society.

*Here's an interesting volume: 'Gadaffi's Libya' by Jonathan Bearman – and of
course you had the doubtful distinction of meeting Gadaffi in Libya. What
impression did he make on you?*

A big impression – I think he's the strangest man I have ever met in my
life. This is the only book I've read that gives a clear and scholarly
examination of Gadaffi and Libya. Gadaffi invited me over to write his
biography but nothing came of it. This is a very serious book that not
only points out the problems that Gadaffi and Libya have but shows how
they developed, and it's analytical and not propagandist or emotional. I'd
recommend it to anyone who wants to know what is happening in Libya.
I think he is a fascinating study of how a person is driven off the rails by
anti-propaganda. I have this curious theory that all the crazy people of
history were actually driven crazy by the reaction of smug allies. I think
Hitler himself was crazy from the start but I think his craziness was
intensified by the smug reaction of the Western Alliance. I think Gadaffi
is painted as a madman. He is not mad but a brilliant subtle person in his
speech and everything else. I was very impressed by this and I said this
was a fascinating personality, not to approve or disapprove of him but to
examine what has made that personality. I'd love to do it some time.

You read a lot of Irish fiction and I see John McGahern's novel 'Amongst Women' on your shelves.

I think it's one of the great modern Irish novels, and I still don't know how he wrote it. I've read it a couple of times and I apply a film analogy to it in asking, 'Where are the cuts?' In a film, if you see the cut there's something wrong with it. In that book I can't find the cuts, the seam. I read McGahern and Banville, although they are very different writers, and I'm in awe at their control of words and how they balance them. It would take some kind of genius to film *Amongst Women*. I don't care for films that are made of books, because it's a horse of a completely different colour. It bears, usually, no relation to the book and doesn't complement or flatter the book. I would hate to see a film being made of *Amongst Women* because it is such a beautiful book. Of John Banville's work I sometimes dip into *Mephisto* because he writes prose like a poet. To see the way he handles words leaves me aghast and I often wonder how many people, like myself, have the neck to sit down and write when there are people like McGahern and Banville writing so perfectly.

Over the years you have been fascinated by the way world cultures and indeed Christianity have influenced Irish society and the way we are. I see Paul Johnson's 'History of Christianity' on your shelves. What's so special about that book?

I suppose that would be the equivalent of my bible, because Christianity has been such a tremendous force in our civilisation and not just our shabby falling-apart civilisation. If you think of how it has rationalised the most dreadful things in the history of this continent and the American continent you here find out where it went wrong or right, what is bad or good about it. I've been fascinated by religion for over thirty years and I've made many films in the religious arena. So when I was doing a series called *Atlantean* there was a tremendous dimension of the history of religion to it. I found Paul Johnson, who is a reactionary old devil, in his *History of Christianity* writes a wonderful history I still refer to. I have another book here, a sort of companion volume to Johnson, and it is called *The Dead Sea Scrolls and the Christian Myth*, by John Marco

Allegro. He was a maverick I met on the Isle of Man a few years ago. His writings are hated by the formal scholars because he broke ranks on the Dead Sea Scrolls which had been taken over by the scholars. He was one of the scholars who was invited to examine the Dead Sea Scrolls and he published about them. He got impatient when he discovered everybody was keeping the lid on the findings and he broke out and wrote. He wrote about the origins of the Jesus story and how it tended to precede our historical version of it. He traced it back to the Essenes in the desert, and if anybody wants to worry about their Christian faith they should read this book *The Dead Sea Scrolls and the Christian Myth*.

38

AUGUSTINE MARTIN

Augustine Martin was Professor of Anglo-Irish Literature in University College Dublin until his untimely death in October 1995. He was a former member of Seanad Éireann where he represented the National University of Ireland. He lectured widely on Irish literature abroad and was conferred with an Honorary Doctor of Laws by the University of St Thomas, New Brunswick. He was Director of the Yeats International Summer School and a member of the Board of the Abbey Theatre. He was Director of the James Joyce International Summer School and a member of the Governing Board of UCD since 1969. His publications include *James Stephens – A Critical Study*, *Yeats: A Life*, *Collected Poems of W. B. Yeats* (Editor), *James Joyce, the Artist and the Labyrinth* (Editor) and several text books for schools. He was a frequent broadcaster on radio and television and a distinguished critic and reviewer.

Augustine Martin, since you are Professor of Anglo-Irish Literature and Drama, I'm not at all surprised to see you have a wall of books on the two great giants of Irish literature, Yeats and Joyce.

I suppose I'm a bit schizophrenic about them. I would have said up to three or four years ago that Yeats was my absolute favourite writer since Shakespeare. Since then I'm turning more towards Joyce, so I'm split between the two. What people often do not realise is the extraordinary correspondence between these two writers, because they worked in the same town, grew up in the same culture and, in a sense, they divided it between them. There is a hell of a lot more of Yeats in Joyce and Joyce in Yeats than appears to the naked eye. One feeds off the other in the reading of them. There are times when I can't bear to read another book of criticism on Yeats or Joyce. I'm basically a primary-text man. I haven't read as much criticism of Joyce as I should, perhaps, but I'd hate to have to read a lot of it, because the jargon in which it is written is sheer agony to read. Joyce has attracted some of the worst and most appalling schools of criticism to him. The Yeatsians are much better. The difference is this: people who are fascinated by Joyce nowadays are fascinated with linguistic matters and they tend to be interested in deconstruction, in feminism and a whole series of -isms in modern criticism, whereas people who are interested in Yeats are fascinated by the reading that he did, all that neo-Plationism, magic, hermitism and all those extraordinary books that he had at his disposal. It's a different kind of adventure reading Yeats criticism from reading Joyce criticism, but by and large I prefer to read the men themselves.

Moving away from Yeats and Joyce, I see you have a lot of biographies on your shelves, including a recent biography of Anthony Trollope by Victoria Glendinning.

This is a marvellous book. As I'm writing a life of Patrick Kavanagh I read a lot of biographies, so I've recently reviewed this biography of Trollope and also biographies of Shaw and Lawrence and Wilde. I am fascinated by biography and I think, as I get older, I'm going to read more biography than fiction. I would say in some cases you learn a lot about the biographer when reading biography – you learn a lot about Ellmann when reading his kind of biography. Victoria Glendinning, on the other hand, tells us a lot about Trollope but you also learn an extraordinary amount about the nineteenth century, and the things that were happening are often unbelievable. For instance, I discovered that they never taught them anything in public schools: they just got them to learn a little Latin by heart. I discovered that the physical practice of homosexuality was perfectly condoned until the middle of the nineteenth century. Even the definition of homosexuality as a category of experience came quite late in that century. She tells you quite amazing things about what people did, what they wore and why, what they ate and how they cooked. This biography of Trollope is also a social history of the nineteenth century, a wonderfully vivacious book.

You mentioned that you are immersed in writing the biography of Patrick Kavanagh, and I see 'Tarry Flynn' and 'The Green Fool', the 'Collected Poems' and everything Kavanagh wrote on your shelves. Why Patrick Kavanagh?

I just adore him. I think *Tarry Flynn* is the novel I have read most often – I think I've read it more often than *The Crock of Gold* by James Stephens. *The Green Fool* is also a marvellous book. I suppose the attraction is the manner in which Kavanagh speaks with a naked honesty out of a rural culture which has never found proper expression before. I think it is quite magical the way his small body of poetry and prose does that. Also, it chimes with my own background, because I come from a rural small town, Leitrim, and it is very similar drumlin country with that ferocious intimacy of experience. You know those lines of his from *The Great Hunger*:

> From every second hill a neighbour watches
> With all the sharpened interest of rivalry.

There's a sense in which you can't do anything without being seen or having to account for it in some mysterious way. Kavanagh catches that almost incestuous way of life which in a way is fading but which will always be there, just as the way people in Dublin spoke is always there in Joyce – but that Joycean dialect will soon be gone under the powerful force of television.

You have a lot of poetry on your shelves by Irish, English and American poets. What are the volumes which you treasure?

Apart from Yeats and Shakespeare my favourite American poets are John Crowe Ransom and Robert Frost. With regard to Irish poets I read them all but John Montague is the Irish poet I think I read most often, next to Patrick Kavanagh, because of his extraordinary accessibility. He manages the heart's affections with supreme honesty and is supremely good on sexual relations and marriage. His poetry on Eros in general is the most courageous and humane of almost any poetry written today.

When you're not reading professionally but want to relax I suspect you indulge in some of the writers I see next on your shelves – John Le Carré, Ed McBain and Raymond Chandler.

These are mostly what I read myself to sleep with. I find the good ones like Chandler you can read over and over again. Le Carré I discovered recently when I broke my ankle and a friend brought me in the latest by a writer I had tried years ago but couldn't make it with because I started with *A Small Town in Germany*. I started Le Carré again and I've read everything by him right through and I'm all set to read him again. He appeals to me as a spinner of yarns, a creator of characters and a writer of English. I think there is hardly anybody who can match him as a prose stylist or as a master of English prose.

I see you have the Catholic novels of François Mauriac alongside novels by Evelyn Waugh and Graham Greene.

I read Mauriac as an undergraduate and he absolutely enthralled me because I was a very committed and intense Catholic then. I'm still a Catholic but I'm more relaxed than I was in those days. Mauriac is a very demanding writer but his exploration of the Catholic conscience – he is almost Jansenistic – and the intensity of his exploration of the history of the human soul is unequaled by either Waugh or Greene. When I re-read a novel like *The River of Fire*, I found it just as compelling as when I read it for the first time.

Here's an Irish writer who is not fully appreciated – Elizabeth Bowen.

She's a great favourite of mine. I think her Irish novel *The Last September* is among the half-dozen great Irish novels. It's quite a remarkable book about the Black and Tan War and the fall of the great houses in the south of Ireland, based on her own home, Bowen's Court. Her English novel like *The Death of the Heart*, about the loss of innocence, are also most poignant. I remember the late Patrick Boyle saying to me, 'Everybody has one book in him,' and he said that it was about the loss of innocence. Everybody can write that one story about coming to maturity or leaving the world of innocent childhood, and if you can write at all you can make that stick. I don't know anybody who has done it better than Elizabeth Bowen.

Among our contemporaries I see you have almost everything written by John McGahern and John Banville, two very different writers.

They are two sophisticates in quite different senses. McGahern masquerades as a kind of rude country writer on the outside, his art concealing art, but his sensibility is so modern. I'm not surprised that his work has been translated successfully into French and that he is a great favourite with the French intellectuals. He is looking at a very traditional rural Leitrim background with a modern sensibility. Banville is a post-modernist writer with so much topspin on his writing you really have to get up early in the morning to stay with his work. If I had to pick one book by each writer I'd go for John McGahern's *Amongst Women* and from John Banville I think I prefer *Copernicus* to *The Book of Evidence*.

Moving away from Ireland, who in contemporary fiction do you read with pleasure?

I have a particular interest in those witty reflexive modern English writers like Julian Barnes, John Fowles and Peter Ackroyd, who are in the tradition of wit and manners which goes right back to Jane Austen and beyond. They have a kind of modern complexity that delights me. They can write a modern novel which encapsulates the complexity of a whole past, like John Fowles's *The French Lieutenant's Woman* which is both a Victorian and modern novel at the same time. Other examples of that genre are Fowles's *The Magus* or Julian Barnes's *Flaubert's Parrot*. I find the way these writers can encapsulate a past into the present in a very sophisticated form of writing absolutely enchanting.

Both the author and publisher's are grateful to the following for permission to reproduce materials used in this book.

The Dedalus Press for 'Hoof Taps' by Tom Mac Intyre; Allen Figgis & Co. Ltd., for 'Good Souls to Survive' by Brendan Kennelly.

OTHER TITLES
from
BLACKWATER PRESS